TRUMP

The Best Golf Advice
I Ever Received

Also by Donald J. Trump

Trump: The Way to the Top
Trump: The Art of the Deal
Trump: Surviving at the Top
Trump: The Art of the Comeback
The America We Deserve
Trump: How to Get Rich

TRUMP

The Best
Golf Advice
I Ever Received

DONALD J. TRUMP

Crown Publishers / New York

Library of Congress Cataloging-in-Publication Data
Trump, Donald J., 1946–
    The best golf advice I ever received / Donald J. Trump.—1st ed.
    1. Golf—Anecdotes.   I. Title.
        GV967.T823   2005
        796.352—dc22   2005003654

ISBN 0-307-20999-7

Printed in the United States of America

Design by Barbara Sturman

10 9 8 7 6 5 4 3 2 1

First Edition

Acknowledgments

I am most grateful to:

Dana Beck, Michael Harder, John Frew and Kevin Sniffen of the Hamilton Group, Adler Robin Books and Jeanne Welsh, Alice Yashinsky, Ed Randall, Jeff Wallach, Bob Whitbread of Caddybytes.com, Michael Patrick Shiels, Mickey Herskowitz, Norma Foerderer and Bernard Diamond of The Trump Organization, and the staff of Bill Adler Books, Inc., for their invaluable help in making this book possible.

Contents

Golf 101
•

7

Home on the Range
●

Get a Grip
●

In the Swing
•

Golf 201
•

In the Zone
•

Get Tough
•

Game Time
•

Mergers and Mulligans
•

Golf 301
•

A Cure for the Yips

•

An Unspoiled Walk
•

Introduction

DONALD J. TRUMP

For me and millions of people—men, women, young and old around the world—golf is more than a game. It is a passion.

For this book, I have personally asked famous and legendary professional golfers, respected golf teachers and coaches, professional caddies, well-known athletes and celebrities, talented architects who have designed some of the world's most impressive courses, and leading executives to share with us in their "own words" the best golf advice they have ever received.

I believe their words will help all of us enjoy the game of golf more.

With our own Trump golf courses, which are among the best in the world, and our well-known golf tournaments, we have contributed to the joys of golf for millions of people.

I believe the book will help to improve your game and add to the pleasure of the game for you and your friends.

Have fun—and a hole in one!

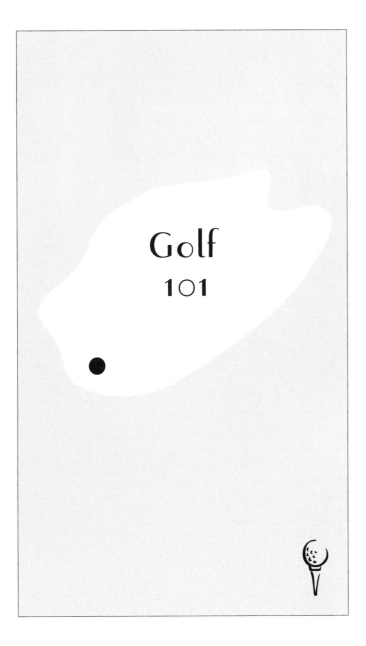

Golf
1O1

Molly BANEY

Golf for Women *Magazine Top 50 Teacher*

I could have saved years of effort if only someone had told me in the beginning to do five things:

1. Count the Cost

The time, physical energy, practice, money, and emotional energy that are required to build a golf game are usually underestimated even by great athletes who take up the game. Be prepared for a process that takes lots of time, patience, and perseverance.

2. Seek an Excellent Golf Teaching Professional

Focus on the fundamentals, not the "quick fixes"

Build your game right the first time with a teacher who will create a golf swing that is built to last. This takes more effort at first, but it is worth it in the long run. Many golf teachers simply "Band-Aid" your game until it falls apart again. You can waste years with Band-Aids and quick fixes, only to be filled with anguish and frustration. There is only a small percentage of teaching professionals who understand cause and effect and can build a solid golf swing from the ground up. A swing that offers maximum consistency and power. A swing customized to your individual body type, learning style, personality, and fitness level. A swing that begins with excellent fundamentals in the preswing foundation of alignment, grip, ball position, stance, and balanced posture.

3. Practice Fundamentals Until You Develop Mastery

Don't take up the game if you do not have the time to practice. Practice can be as simple as twenty minutes a day in your backyard hitting plastic golf balls. In your living room, you can practice the fundamentals of grip, alignment, posture, and preswing setup routines. A golf professional who builds your game from the ground up will give you drills to practice. You don't always have to be at the driving range to make progress with your game. The important thing is to practice drills consistently.

4. Visualize Your Success

To reach your goals at the fastest rate, spend time each day thinking about playing the golf of your dreams. Imagine the future reality you wish to experience while playing golf. Picture your ideal golf swing, ideal round of golf, low scores, and tournament wins. Celebrate it as if it has already happened.

5. For Maximized Performance, Use the Best Equipment

After building the fundamentals of your golf swing, seek a certified professional club fitter and purchase custom-fit golf clubs. In addition to your golf clubs, consider the fifteenth club in your golf bag which is your "Golf Body." Maximize your potential as a golfer by following a customized golf fitness and flexibility program as outlined by a certified golf fitness expert or physical therapist.

Joe Louis BARROW Jr.

Executive Director, The First Tee

Golf has very much been a part of my life. I was first introduced to the game by my father, Joe Louis, when I was very young. There is a photo floating around showing me placing a ball on a tee when I was three or four years old. I remember very clearly missing the tee many times and finally my dad reaching over to help me with his huge hands, saying, "Son, this is how you do it."

My dad loved the game. Ed Sullivan introduced him to golf in 1935. In fact, some say the reason he lost to Max Schmeling in 1936 was because he was spending more time on the golf course than training for the fight. Max knocked him out in the twelfth round. I do believe that was my dad's most important fight because it taught him a very critical lesson—never take victory for granted. That loss also taught him perseverance.

Perseverance makes perfect

One of the key values we share with young people at The First Tee is perseverance, which includes lessons about the importance of staying focused and the discipline of planning, setting goals, and working to achieve them step-by-step. We have reached more than four hundred thousand young people in a very short period of time. To see the increased confidence of the participants at The First Tee and their ability to learn to trust their judgment have been most gratifying to the thousands of individuals sharing and teaching The First Tee life skills educational experience.

I learned a great deal from my dad on the golf course. It was the only time we were able to spend private time together. He loved the game, engaging with others, competing,, and enjoying the interaction and camaraderie.

And, yes, Joe Louis was known to make a wager or two on the golf course (a lesson we do not share with the young people at The First Tee). In the end, my dad would tell me, "Son, there are only two holes you need to play well—nine and eighteen." In most instances, the bets were settled on nine and eighteen. My friends who I have played golf with over the years have said that's a lesson I learned well from my dad.

Norm CROSBY

Entertainer

I host several tournaments for the Muscular Dystrophy Association and for the City of Hope. I have golf shirts, golf bags, and golf gloves that are inscribed "Norm Crosby Golf Classic," "Norm Crosby Celebrity Invitational," and so on, but I am a terrible golfer.

For many years, I have been invited to the Frank Sinatra Celebrity Invitational Golf Tournament, the Kraft Nabisco

Championship, and many others because the sponsors want me to be in the show. I host the MDA event because I am a cohost on the Jerry Lewis Telethon and I host the City of Hope Classic because I am in my twentieth year as the Ambassador of Good Will for the City of Hope.

My golf game is deplorable, if not worse.

I am constantly on the road and have very little time to play or practice between tournaments; therefore, I receive advice from almost everyone who sees me hit a ball.

Some golfers hear some very encouraging remarks after they hit: "You're going to love it!" or "That's a golf shot!" or something similar. When I hit, they say, "Sounded good!" or "I think it opens up over there!"

I played with Patty Sheehan at the LPGA Nabisco Dinah Shore the year she was inducted into the LPGA Hall of Fame. She was wonderful and very generous with her advice. After a few holes and several suggestions, she finally said, "Norm, why don't you take a few lessons and then *quit!*"

Lee Trevino, one of the very best of the great pro golfers, had a television show called *Golf for Swingers,* and I was invited to play against Lawrence Welk. It was a great day, and Lee and I became friends.

I asked him if he ever got nervous making a putt on the eighteenth hole that might be worth a million dollars in prize money. He

Take a few lessons then *quit*!

replied, "Not at all, but years ago when I was playing a guy for fifty bucks and I was lining up the winning putt knowing that I only had four dollars in my pocket . . . that's when I was nervous!"

John C. CUSHMAN III

Chairman, Cushman & Wakefield, Inc.

I play a lot of golf in the Grand Teton area of Idaho and Wyoming. These areas are known for their elk and moose populations. While playing one day, I sliced my drive into the woods and it ended up beside a grazing moose. My playing partner advised, "Take a mulligan—never argue with a moose over ball possession!"

Brad FAXON

Seven PGA Tour Championships
Two-Time Ryder Cup Team Member

Having been on the tour for twenty-two years, I have had my share of golf tips! It is hard to pick one that is the best, but I did get some advice from Bob Rotella, the noted sports psychologist, that has helped me as much as any tip I can remember.

What he said was amazingly simple, but can be difficult to do. He said that a confident golfer is one who knows where the ball is going before he hits it! So, no matter what level you are, if you think about where you want the ball to go, then you can't help but get better. Remember, no matter what your handicap is, it will always help to think about the ball going toward your target.

> **Visualize your target before you hit the ball**

That is the best tip I have ever received!

David FEHERTY

Ryder Cup Team Member
Former European Tour Player
Golf Analyst, CBS Sports

The best golf advice I've ever received was given to me by Gary McCord. He told me to give up competitive golf and go into television!

Shelby FUTCH

Founder and President, John Jacobs' Golf Schools
President, Golf Digest Schools
Golf Magazine *Top 50 Teacher*

My father won a set of Bobby Jones clubs in a poker game in West Texas when I was in the fifth grade. We lived twenty-eight miles from the nearest town and sixty miles from the nearest golf course. The bag of clubs did not include a golf ball, and the only thing we had was a softball and a tennis ball. In fact, we didn't know there was such a thing as a golf ball. I played the tennis ball around the wheat fields where I lived for about a year before we moved to Ponca City, Oklahoma. I was in the seventh grade by then. The school made an announcement that anyone who wanted to try out for the golf team should meet Saturday at the local course that was ten miles away. I rode my bicycle with the clubs over my shoulder and one tennis ball.

Always use a golf ball

There was no driving range in those days, so you went to the first tee and did the best you could. I walked up to the first tee, put my tennis ball on the ground, and gave it my best hit. Coach Cassingham walked over and asked if I was joking and discovered I wasn't. He then gave me a real live golf ball to hit. I had a couple of goes at it before connecting because it was so small. When I hit it, I was amazed at how far it went. Never mind how far off line—it went so far!

I went on to win more than forty tournaments in Oklahoma and Texas and received a golf scholarship to Oklahoma State. My brother, Ron, followed me and won most of the same tournaments and played on the University of Arkansas golf team. My father and mother had never graduated from high school, and they wanted their two sons to attend college. This would have been a hardship for them, but a set of golf clubs won during a poker game, valued at $25, got us both through school.

So the best advice I ever received was . . . use a golf ball instead of a tennis ball!

Tom GLAVINE

New York Mets

Quit the game. No, actually, the best advice I probably ever got was to relax and just play the golf course. Don't get caught up in your score trying to make birdies or making up for bogeys. Just play the golf course and take what it gives you.

Dick HUFF

PGA Professional, Las Vegas Paiute Golf Resort

After many years of taking lessons, reading golf instructional publications, and viewing slow-motion films of the swing and learning proper grip, good posture, alignment, ball placement, correct swing plane during the back and forward swing, correct weight transfer, and balance, I was having moderate success as a collegiate golfer at Florida State University in the mid-1950s.

I wrote the great Sam Snead, who wintered in Boca Raton, Florida, a letter asking if I could stop by for a lesson on my way home during a semester break. He answered that he would be happy to help me, but he said in his letter, "Dick, remember, there is no substitute for hard work!"

Work harder, play better

This advice has always remained with me, and I have passed it along to hundreds of my most serious students over the years.

Hale IRWIN

Three-Time U.S. Open Winner
Five-Time Ryder Cup Team Member
Forty Champions Tour Titles
World Golf Hall of Fame

The best golf advice I ever received came from my deceased father. His only shortcoming was that he didn't live long enough to see it fully implemented. His advice and encouragement were to never settle for anything less than what you can truly achieve. The fact is that the good things in life, which we hold dear, are not going to come easily. Hard work, sacrifice, and dedication are only a few of the ingredients in that formula for success.

Those are only words to some, but they have lived with me for many years. My wish is that others will embrace them as I have.

Russ LEWIS

CEO, New York Times Company

When teeing off, don't stand too close to the ball after you've hit it.

Arnold PALMER

Four Masters Titles
1960 U.S. Open Champion
Two-Time British Open Champion
Six-Time Ryder Cup Team Member (Two-Time Captain)
Four-Time Vardon Trophy Winner
Ten Champions Tour Titles
World Golf Hall of Fame

The best golf advice I ever received came when I was just three years old. My father, who was the golf pro and course superintendent at our hometown Latrobe Country Club, was introducing me to the game. He had cut down and re-gripped a women's club for me. He wrapped his big, strong hands over mine and showed me how to hold the club with the Vardon, or overlapping, grip. He told me that was the right way to grip a club and not to change it. I never did.

Hit it hard

Then, Pap told me something that developed into the style that has been my way of playing the game ever since. He said, "Hit it hard, boy. Go find the ball and hit it hard again." Some people have said that there were times during my career when I was too aggressive, but I know that I won a lot of tournaments and lost very few playing that way.

Reilley RANKIN

LPGA Tour Player

My dad's way of introducing me to a game he loved so much were words I often heard and are now the greatest golf advice I ever received. He always said, "Let her learn to love the game and then teach her how to play." These words became the foundation of my dreams. Not only was I given the opportunity to explore my childhood, but more important, I was given the freedom to discover and embrace the passion I had for the game of golf.

Burt REYNOLDS

Actor

The best golf advice I ever received was when my Jupiter neighbor, the great Jack Nicklaus, said, "Maybe you should think about taking up another sport."

Robert A. REYNOLDS Jr.

Chairman, President, and CEO,
Graybar Electric Company

The best golf advice I ever received was from my spouse: Remember, it's only a game.

Darius RUCKER

Musician

The best golf advice that I have ever gotten was from the great Payne Stewart. We were playing in the first VH1 Pro-Am together. I wasn't playing too well, and after one real bad shot I shouted something profane and put my club in the bag with a bit of aggression. Payne walked over to me, put his arm around me, and said, "Until they pay you to play, just enjoy the game." Then, as he walked away, he turned, smiled, and jokingly said, "You're not good enough to get that pissed off."

The other great piece of advice that comes to mind is something that is said to me when I play with Tiger: "Bring your money!"

Stephanie SPARKS

Host, The Golf Channel's Golf with Style
Former LPGA Tour Player

There is something about a new pair of sneakers that makes you feel like you can jump higher, run faster. When I was little, every time I would get a new pair of shoes, I would challenge my big sister to a race. As I pulled my new blue-and-gold Zips from the box, I just knew these were the shoes that would finally take me to victory.

Huffing and puffing, I made my way toward the imaginary finish line adjacent to the mailbox, only to see the back of my sister's head as she crossed it. The shoes did not work; she had won again.

My grandmother had the same view on her golf clubs. She just knew she would hit it straighter and hit it farther with a new set of shiny clubs. To disprove her theory, my grandfather took out her old, beat-up set of ladies clubs, and proceeded to shoot his age—69.

Don't rely on your equipment to carry your game

The lesson I learned at a very early age is that the equipment can only get you so far . . . the rest is up to you.

Home on
the Range

Ernie BARBOUR

PGA Instructor, The Bridges Golf Club,
San Ramon, California

As a PGA golf professional, I have had so many wonderful experiences in my golf journey. One of the most powerful was nine or ten years ago when I met a fellow professional named Fred Shoemaker. As a busy head pro, teacher, tournament coordinator, and so on, I found myself swallowed up by the industry of golf and all my growing responsibilities.

Try playing the course with one club

As an avid reader and historian of golf, my curiosity led me to pick up Fred's book, *Extraordinary Golf.* It was a great alternative approach to playing and enjoying golf. Not long after reading the book, I went to a seminar and workshop with Fred and felt afterward a new energy about myself, my coaching, and relating to others, and I discovered that being on the golf course can present so much more than I thought.

One of Fred's suggestions was to go on the golf course in the evening and walk three, six, or nine holes carrying only one golf club—any club, but only one. After a couple of months of pondering such a silly notion, I did it!

On a warm summer evening, I chose a seven iron and went to the first tee alone. The first hole was a 360-yard dogleg par 4 and, while looking down the fairway, I realized that a nice 8- or 10-yard draw might give me a few extra yards of roll. Off I went. When I finally reached the green, I had to figure out how to most effectively putt with a seven iron and, wow, the adventures and exploration of using my imagination had begun. After playing five or six holes that evening, I found myself having to create short lofted seven-iron pitches, short bunker shots, bump and runs, high short fades, and on and on. As I came off the eighth tee, I found myself looking up at a pink, orange, and lavender sunset and staring at a family of ducks playing together in the pond by the green. Things I'm not sure I paid much attention to over the years.

A couple of weeks went by, and at the conclusion of an all-day youth junior golf camp, I had the boys join me in walking nine holes. All the moms dropped them off and, with their little bags over their shoulders, they walked over to my car trunk and watched me rifle through my big Titleist Staff Bag, pull out a six iron, take one ball and my glove, and close the trunk. "Let's go have some fun," I told them. On the first tee I said, "Hey, guys, I think I'll hit a six iron here," and off we went. After a few holes, one of the boys asked me why I was doing this. My response was simply that it was great fun to be creative, to use my mind, my eyes, and my old skills, along with creating some new skills, to pull out the best that I have and that the score this evening just didn't matter. Before that nine holes was over, I had the kids watching squirrels chase each other up trees and hitting bump-and-run six irons with me from forty yards off the green.

I've shared that advice with thousands of my students around the world, and soon after meeting Fred I became a full-time teacher and coach of golf and more! This alternative way of seeing and playing golf helped me "learn how to learn."

Bill DAVIS

PGA Master Professional,
Jupiter Hills Golf Club, Tequesta, Florida

Ken Venturi told me to practice by what I was getting done, not by how long it was taking. Good players should always spend most of their practice on the course with a real target.

Rebecca DENGLER

Golf for Women *Magazine Top 50 Teacher*

Early on in my golf career I learned how to chip. I was working on the ground crew at a local private club and the assistant professional offered to help me out. I asked him to show me how to chip. He proceeded to give me a seven iron and told me to hit it like a putt. Well, I did, and I proceeded to chip in within the first few attempts. The ball hopped a little and rolled right next to or into the hole. I looked at him and asked, "Is that it?" And he replied, "Yes." Since then, that simple explanation has had one of the biggest impacts on my career as a teacher in learning how to keep things simple. Teaching others to chip is one of the easiest lessons I know of. Most average players would be better off with this simple chip that rolls to the hole than a more complicated shot that they try to get up in the air and land and bring to a stop near the hole.

Jim FURYK

2003 U.S. Open Champion
Four-Time Ryder Cup Team Member

The best advice came from my father, who was a golf pro when I was a child and still to this day is my only teacher.

Early on, he taught me one really important thing. Most mistakes that we make in a golf shot, whether as an amateur or as a golf professional, are made before the swing—either in the setup or preshot routine. Because of that, I work very, very hard—even harder—on my preshot and my setup than I do on my swing. Which, looking at my swing, may seem quite apparent.

The alignment consists of a lot of things—grip, posture, ball position. When I was young, my father harped on me to work on the alignment. He told me to put some clubs down parallel to my target line to help keep my shoulders parallel in order to make sure I was aligned well. My bad habit has always been to aim left. When I was growing up, this caused me to hit a very big cut—even a borderline slice. Although my father wanted me to put those clubs down during practice sessions, like most kids I was stubborn (and maybe a little lazy) and I didn't always do it. So my alignment suffered, and I aimed left quite often.

By the late 1990s, I got fed up with being inconsistent in my setup. So every practice session I started carrying rulers around in my bag, making sure I put them down parallel to my target line every time. Doing this allowed me to practice my alignment on every swing I made during practice. And the results have definitely shown—I'm a much more consistent ball striker, both in terms of confidence and statistics, than I was early in my career.

Most mistakes are made before the swing

Now I get to return the favor because my dad's the stubborn one and doesn't like to put the rulers down. He carries them in his bag when he practices but usually doesn't use them. So now I harp on him—he's getting better about it, and hopefully his game will improve, too.

Fred GIBSON

Champions Tour Player

During my first year as an exempt player on the Champions Tour, I had the privilege of getting to know Gary Player. I played several tournament rounds with him and had the opportunity to spend time with Gary on the practice range. He gave me one piece of advice that has stayed with me for the past six years on the Champions Tour. Gary mentioned that years earlier he had asked Ben Hogan how to be successful in golf and that Hogan asked him whether he practiced a lot. Gary replied, "Yes."

Hogan then replied, "Well, then,

Double your practice time

double it."

Now, for a story.

Toward the end of my first year on the PGA Senior Tour, we were playing in Napa Valley at the Silverado Resort. After the first round on Friday and prior to dinner, I returned to the course to practice my bunker shots. The sand trap was directly behind the practice tee, and on the other side of the bunker, in front of the guest suites, there was a cocktail reception attended by a number of the best-known players of the event.

As I was practicing, one of the players yelled out to me that I could get fined for wearing jeans on the course grounds, including the practice area, as this was against the rules. No sooner had that player finished when Bob Murphy yelled over to me, "Fred, keep practicing, and if something happens I'll pay the fine!"

John HOBBINS

Founder, Greenside Golf Academy

As a golf instructor, I must build my teaching technique on a foundation that is irrefutable. In doing so, I am able to convey to the student an understanding of what happens with the swinging of a golf club. Golfers study the golf swing with the hope of making their swing produce a better ball flight. In order to improve the flight of a golf ball, a golfer has to improve the motion of the golf club. In order to improve the motion of the golf club, the golfer must improve his or her body motion. It is the motion of the body that controls the club that controls the ball flight. With this premise in mind, I structure my teaching on the notion of moving the body in a manner that will create an arc with a swinging motion of the golf club.

It's all about the arc

A golfer stands to the side of a golf ball in the same manner that a tennis player or a baseball hitter stands to the side of the ball he or she wants to strike. Any time an individual stands to the side of an object that he or she wants to hit, his or her swinging motion must be on an arc. A golf club, a tennis racket, and a baseball bat are all swinging on an arc, though in different planes. In learning or improving a golf swing, it is necessary to make the correct body movements that allow the golf club the greatest possibility of being swung on an arc around the body. It is this movement that eludes most golfers. Proper contact with a golf ball is a result of a golf club swinging on arc. A straight golf shot is a result of the golf club being swung on an arc. All too often, golfers fail to understand this premise.

Golfers attempt to swing the golf club down the target line. This provides them a linear motion that does not have an application in a good golf swing. Observe the swing of any talented player and you will see that his or her swinging motion works away from the ball and back to the ball and through to the finish on an inclined arc. I liken it to the shape of a Ferris wheel that has been tilted on its side. A Ferris wheel would sit in a vertical position at ninety degrees. If that were tilted to a forty-five-degree angle, you would have the correct shape of an arc for a good golf swing. Once you understand this premise, then you can begin to make the necessary changes in your body motion that will allow your golf club to travel on arc around your body.

I learned this through my association with Jim Hardy and Mike LaBauve, and it has become a cornerstone of my teaching. Once a student trains his or her body to swing the club on arc, he or she finds solid contact and improved ball flight.

Roberta ISLEIB

Agatha and Anthony-Nominated Author of
Six Strokes Under, A Buried Lie, Putt to Death,
and Fairway to Heaven

Find a teaching professional you really click with and take lessons. Everyone learns a little differently, and you'll have to look around for the teacher that "speaks your language."

I know a lot about this; in fact, my whole writing career started with bad golf.

When I met my husband-to-be more than ten years ago, I was a tennis player—not a golfer. To me, golf ranked right up there with drag racing and bowling as one of the most boring sports ever invented. But you remember how new love goes. He invited me out to play a few holes and then I got hooked—on both of them, of course. Let's face it, though, I was a slow learner— an expert on whiffs, nicks, and worm-endangering grounders.

Find a golf pro who's right for you

One day we played eighteen holes with another couple, and I was having my usual challenging round, torturing myself and the rest of the foursome. After we'd finished and were sitting on the porch with a beer, the other man turned to me and said, "For God's sake, Roberta, take a lesson!"

Well, I had been taking lessons. But I took more lessons. I "knew" that I should flex my knees, take the club away inside, never ever go past parallel, put my elbow in my pocket, and swing out to right field. This jumble of verbal instructions translated into a cramped ball-slashing as I worked my way through eight teaching professionals. I finally got it when my last teacher combined visual cues with the words.

And then I had my first article published: "Choosing Your Pro!" You can understand that I had developed into an expert in the field.

So take a lesson! If you're like me, you may have to take more than one. And stay with it until you find the pro that speaks your language.

Brad JAMES

Head Coach, Men's Golf,
University of Minnesota

Spend 90 percent of your time practicing from one hundred yards and in.

Meg MALLON

Two-Time U.S. Women's Open Champion
Eighteen LPGA Tour Titles

I am always asked the question, how many hours a day do you practice? Many people believe that if you just hit balls all day on the range you will naturally become a better player. Well, from my experience, this couldn't be further from the truth.

The best advice I have ever received was from my teacher of seventeen years, Mike McGetrick. He taught me that the quality of your practice is far more important than the quantity. When I practice, I have a target and a goal for every shot. This gives me constant feedback on whether I need to fix something or whether I can go ahead and groove what

> **Treat every practice shot like a game shot**

I'm doing well. Rather than aimlessly pounding ball after ball, I treat every shot as though I were in a game situation. This has helped me for the big stage when the time comes. I have utilized this advice for my entire career and truly feel it has helped me have a long and successful golfing life.

Rick MARTINO

Director of Instruction, PGA of America

When students ask you to become their coach, they are committing to you more than their athletic abilities and time—they bring their hopes and dreams!

Rick McCORD

Golf Magazine Top 100 Teacher

The best advice I could give a golfer from my own personal experience as a player and teacher is to train and educate the hands. They are what control the involuntary response of the body. Example: Stand erect and imagine there is an item on a shelf directly behind you over your right shoulder and you want to grab it off the shelf with your left hand. You will experience how the body responds with a turning motion to accommodate where the hand wants to go.

Mary Beth McGIRR

LPGA Master Professional
Golf for Women *Magazine Top 50 Teacher*

Perhaps the best golf advice I ever received was learning to differentiate between *types* of practice. Since practice is such a key component for improvement, there are many improvement strategies that can be employed. Practicing the right things is what creates good habits in golf.

There are basically two types of practice in golf: traditional practice and practice for transfer.

The traditional type of practice is characterized by repetitions of the same skill. For example, you may be working to groove a particular aspect of

**Practice
like you play**

your short irons. In this case, hitting twenty-five consecutive seven irons would be appropriate and probably helpful. In putting, you often see players repeatedly making short, straight putts to work on their technique and build up their confidence.

At some point, however, variability of practice becomes essential for improvement. This is the component of practice that relates to transfer of learning (taking the skills from the practice tee to the golf course). In golf, as in all sports, it's critical that you practice in such a way that it simulates the conditions of the real game. In the case of golf, the game never demands twenty-five 7 irons in a row. Repetitive practice does have its merits, but at a certain point, you have to put the skill components back into the game. After spending ten minutes of hitting only seven irons, test yourself. Step away, go through your routine on-course setup, and hit only one 7 iron to a specific target. Determine its imaginary outcome.

Another example would be to practice with your driving club. At the end of your traditional practice session, save ten balls and hit them down a predetermined "fairway." Determine what percentage of drives in the fairway is acceptable and compatible with your caliber of skill and experience. Then, as a final test, take one ball, go through your routine, and see if you can hit that drive into the fairway. These are some examples of how you can mix up your practice sessions to make them enjoyable, challenging, and adaptable to the real conditions of the game.

You can also simulate playing a round on the practice tee. Just like in the real game, tee off with your driving club, determine its imagined landing spot, and proceed to hit each shot with the necessary club that you would need. Even mix it up by hitting from some uneven lies and use a practice bunker, if one is available. The mental practice of visualizing golf shots is helpful for your improvement as well!

It's very important that you differentiate between the "golf swing" and the "game of golf." If your objective is to improve some specific component of your swing, then traditional practice is suitable and helpful. However, you must continually incorporate these improved skills into the real game. The reality is that golf is played with one ball and with one shot at a time!

Grace PARK

Six LPGA Tour Titles

Practice, practice, practice. My dad gave me that advice all the time when I was growing up and learning to play. I'd go out and play and practice a little bit when I started, between the ages of ten and twelve. It took a long time for me to understand why I needed to practice every day, but now it's stuck in me.

I do whatever I feel like doing that day. I have my own way of practicing. I don't plan it in advance—I just do whatever comes. It's fun because I imagine the shots and then hit them. And when I practice them enough, I have them when I need them in competition. My dad was right: practice, practice, practice.

David PHILLIPS

Cofounder, Titleist Performance Institute

The best tip I ever received was from my father, who introduced me to this great game in Papua New Guinea when I was twelve years old. My father never pretended to be a great golfer and at his best managed an 8 handicap. As much as he loved to yell support at my golf tournaments and soccer and rugby games, he never attempted to coach me when I was a kid. He always let the coaches do what they were best at. What he did for me was much more valuable and may be the reason I teach and continue to strive to learn as much as I can about golf today. My father knew the value of a coach—the best players in the world have coaches for their swing, as well as the mental and fitness aspects. They don't attempt to figure this game out on their own; it is far too complicated, and there are too many ways to get the job done.

Don't try to figure out the game on your own

If you are serious about getting better at this game, find a PGA golf professional who teaches the game and shows an interest in you and your goals. Put your game in his hands, knowing that at times it will be frustrating and that nothing in life comes without hard work and a clear vision. Remember, you can't see yourself when you swing, and the difference between feel and real will amaze you. Get a coach.

Dicky PRIDE

PGA Tour Player

When you talk about the best golf advice I ever received, it is an easy decision for me. I had just graduated from the University of Alabama and moved to Orlando, Florida, to pursue a career in golf. I fortunately had a friend and former teammate, Alan Pope, who was a member of Arnold Palmer's Bay Hill Club. He arranged for me to have the opportunity to apply for a junior membership. I was fortunate enough to be accepted.

The first day I was a member, Mr. Palmer was practicing on the putting green. I walked over to thank him for allowing me to join. Needless to say, I was as nervous as a twenty-three-year-old would be when he is speaking to one of his idols. In typical Palmer fashion, he was very gracious and asked me about my game and where I wanted to go with it. I told him that I was about to turn professional and my goal was to play and win on the PGA Tour.

You get out of golf what you put into golf

Immediately, Mr. Palmer crouched down a bit and looked me straight in the eyes. He asked me if he could give me some advice about professional golf. I tried to look calm as I said, "Yes, sir." However, I am quite certain that my eyes got very big, and I took a deep breath as if bracing for impact.

He then said, "There are no miracles in this game; you only get out of it what you put into it." I thanked Mr. Palmer for the advice and went into the pro shop. I asked the assistants for a pen and sheet of paper so I could write down what Mr. Palmer had told me. The actual chances of my forgetting what Mr. Palmer had told me were slim to none, but I wrote it down anyway. That sheet of paper still sits on my desk to this day.

I have now been a member of Bay Hill for twelve years. I still seek Mr. Palmer's advice on a number of subjects, but especially golf. He is always gracious and informative. I am truly in debt to him for everything he has done for my family and me. I will always remember the first advice he gave me. It has been the model for my golfing career. In 1994, during my rookie year on the PGA Tour, his advice paid off when I won the FedEx St. Jude Classic.

Dana RADER

Golf Magazine *Top 100 Teacher*

My pro, Joe Cheves, advised me that in order to play the game with any luck and skill, I had to practice. He encouraged me to work hard and wait with great expectation because one doesn't know when one's day in the sun will come.

Justin ROSE

PGA Tour Player
www.kenrosefoundation.com

The best piece of golf advice I have ever been given came from my dad when I was struggling to make the transition from amateur to professional golf in 1998–1999. It didn't come in the form of a technical tip or swing thought, it was more his enabling me to realize what the important things were in order for me to break through barriers, achieve success, and perform to my potential.

As an amateur, I was always regarded as incredibly talented and ahead of the game in terms of age. For example, when I was fourteen, I won the England Under 18 and Under 16 Championships in the same summer, and got to the final stage of Open Qualifying. Success had come very easily to me; therefore, when I stepped into the Big Boys' League, I perhaps didn't expect the transition and the standard to be so challenging. When my dad, who was very close to me, saw my form begin to deteriorate and my beginning to panic because the expected results weren't happening, he knew that then was the time to have a father-to-son chat with me.

In this chat, he reassured me that talent never goes away. However, talent on its own will never be enough to achieve all of your goals; it's work ethic and dedication that are the essential components to back up your talent. He also made me realize that the path to get there can be a long and winding one, and not to expect success to come instantly.

Talent alone is not enough

I put all my trust in practicing hard and, sure enough, my results slowly improved and there was a definite sense of progress. I think this was a telling time in my career because I matured a lot. I also learned that you have to give the game respect, that you never master it, and that you always have to keep your eye on the ball, so to speak!

What I like about my father's advice is that it rings true every time I face a challenge, and it gives me something positive to feed from. Sadly, my dad passed away in September 2002, but he has left me with so much that influences the decisions I make every day.

Leo P. TABICK

Director of Instruction, Golf Performance Academy

The best golf advice I ever received was from Carl Lohren, a PGA professional who wrote *One Move to Better Golf* and *Getting Set for Golf.* This advice on target alignment will benefit players at all levels.

Focus on proper target alignment

If you have been experiencing errant and erratic ball-flight patterns, incorrect target alignment may be a reason. By target alignment, I mean the relationship of your body to the target line. The following drill will help to improve this skill.

On the range, you will need three clubs as alignment tools.

For Right-Handed Players

1. Select a target distance that represents the distance of the golf club used in the drill. (I recommend the eight iron or six iron as the preferred club.)

2. Place the grip end of the first alignment club behind the golf ball, facing your intended target. (Leave room for the clubface of the practice iron for ball striking.)
3. Place the second club parallel to the first alignment club, facing left of the intended target.
4. The third alignment club is placed perpendicular to the golf ball. The grip is facing the ball and the clubface is between the feet.

While looking down at the golf ball, place the clubface of the practice iron behind the ball without touching the alignment clubs. Take your correct stance and posture. Notice the alignment club's position and think of your own body's alignment.

Remember, the shoulders are slightly open, and the hips are square to the alignment clubs.

Main Points

1. Incorporate alignment training into your practice sessions and straighter ball-flight patterns will be a rewarding result.
2. Remember that your upper body needs to be open; having your toes parallel to the target line will enable you to achieve a more desirable path and plane for the golf swing.

Get a
Grip

Tommy BOLT

1958 U.S. Open Champion
Fifteen PGA Tour Titles
Two-Time Ryder Cup Team Member
World Golf Hall of Fame

In 1955, I called Ben Hogan from Sarasota and told him, "Hey, Ben, I'm hooking the ball and I need help." He said to come on down and he'd straighten it out for me.

I went to his home in Fort Worth for a couple of weeks. He moved my left hand over on top of the club and I became a new golfer. I had been on the tour just four or five years when he changed my grip. I was still learning how to play.

Changing your grip can change your game

I won a bunch of tournaments right after that. A month later, we went to San Francisco for the U.S. Open and I led the tournament for two rounds. Hogan and Jack Fleck were tied on the last day—they had a famous playoff and Fleck won it. I finished in a tie for third with Sam Snead.

Ben was a good man and an unselfish one.

Steve BOSDOSH

Golf Magazine *Top 100 Teacher*

Hold the handle of your club more in your fingers. This allows for more feel and more sensitivity for the weight of the clubhead. Make an athletic, tension-free motion without concern for the outcome! This creates a swing of the club with the ball simply getting in the way of the clubhead, not a "hit" at an object. Holding the handle more in the palm creates tension and tension encourages a hit, not a free swing. The more concerned you are about the outcome, the more tension, the more hit, the less swing. This all produces a nonathletic motion. You end up steering the ball around the course. Result: no fun! We all think too much on the course. The swing was never meant to be a series of connect the dots followed by somehow hitting it. The golf swing is just that—a swing! Let it fly. Result: more *fun*!

Michael CARRICK

PGA Tour Caddy (twenty-one years with Tom Kite;
currently caddying for Mark Hensby)
Founder, Professional Caddies Association
Author, Caddie Sense

It is very important to relax. Don't grip the club in a death grip. Tension is one of the biggest destroyers of a good golf swing.

Also, most amateurs don't take enough club for each shot. About 90 percent of golfers (mostly due to male ego) never take enough club for the shot at hand. Once they probably hit their seven iron 155 yards, so now they think it is always a seven from that distance. On the Wednesday pro-ams, I usually give the amateurs about ten yards more when they ask for yardage, and most still come up short.

Jerry HAAS

Head Coach, Men's Golf, Wake Forest University

The best advice I ever received was from my uncle, Bob Goalby, who was the 1968 Masters champion.

He worked with me when I was a young man and constantly stressed the importance of the grip. What a simple thing, yet the most important element if a player wants to get better. I am currently the head golf coach at Wake Forest and still play today. I am glad I listened because he was right— you *can* get better with a good grip. Every time I play, I think of how fortunate I was to have someone show me how to do something properly.

Keep in mind that out of one hundred great golfers, ninety-nine have good grips.

Jim HARDY

Golf Magazine *Top 100 Teacher*
Golf Digest *Top 50 Swing Coach*
Principal, *Jacobsen Hardy Golf Course Design*

My best golf advice came during a bout of severe duck hooking with my driver. I had been trying to stop the hook by holding tight with my left hand and pulling the butt of the club forward. The tighter I held with my left hand, the more I hooked the ball, though I would occasionally hit a straight right push. With so much left-hand grip pressure, I noticed that often my right hand would fly off the club during impact.

John Jacobs, the noted teacher from Great Britain, suggested that I was hooking because my right hand and right side were not coming through the ball; as a result, I was simply slapping the clubface violently closed during impact, causing the duck hook. He had me locate the lifeline on my right palm, exactly where it lies at the base of the

Locate your lifeline

thumb. He told me to squeeze that point against my left thumb, where that point and the left thumb meet, as hard as I could during impact. He even went so far as to place a small pebble between my hands at that intersect point and had me squeeze as hard as if I were trying to bury the pebble in my left thumb.

I could not hook. In fact, the harder I tried to roll my right hand on top of the left hand and over it, the straighter I hit the ball. All I had to do was make sure the pressure between my hands, at that exact intersect point, was strong during impact. My right side was now coming through impact instead of just slapping the ball, and my duck hooks were a thing of the past.

Bruce HEPPLER

Head Coach, Men's Golf,
Georgia Institute of Technology

One of the greatest challenges to hitting a quality shot in a critical moment during competition is the tension created by the situation. There are two very important keys to eliminate the tension that affects the golf swing in these moments. The first is a preshot routine that is developed on the practice tee and followed on every shot, whether it is on the first hole or the seventy-second hole. By getting into the process of planning and preparing for the shot and thinking about the things necessary to execute, the shot will be away before the player has the chance to calculate the costs of a bad swing. This will allow for a swing with positive thoughts. The other key is grip pressure. Tension is transferred from the player to the clubface with hands. As long as a player has light grip pressure, that transfer can't take place. Light grip pressure will allow the player to maintain the rhythm that will permit the proper sequence of the swing to take place. These two fundamentals executed properly will allow the player to perform under any type of pressure.

Kip PUTERBAUGH

PGA Instructor, Aviara Golf Academy

The best advice I ever received was from my first instructor, Paul Runyan. He stressed to me the importance of a proper grip and posture over the ball. He said that if you do not do this properly, you would never establish a fundamentally sound swing. I was very fortunate that when I would be out practicing he'd always walk by in between lessons and correct my grip, posture, or alignment.

As I have progressed through the years as a teacher, I have learned the wisdom of his instruction. In *Harvey Penick's Little Red Book,* the noted teacher stated, "Without the proper grip or posture everything you know about the swing is worthless." What this means is that all instruction is based on the premise that whoever is reading the instruction already has a proper grip and posture. Without these primary fundamentals, nothing that you know about the swing will work. That is why Penick also said, "If you don't have a good grip, don't go looking for a good swing."

> **Grip and posture are fundamental**

Having taught at golf schools for the past seventeen years, plus having given thirty-two years of private instruction, I can tell you that less than 5 percent of my students show up for their first lesson with these two fundamentals established. Although they may be awkward to learn and frustrating to incorporate into your game, they will pay huge dividends to the long-term development of your game.

Joe THEISMANN

NFL Player, 1974–1985
NFL MVP, 1983
Super Bowl Champion, 1983
College Football Hall of Fame

The best advice I ever got had to do with my grip. I use a baseball grip. I don't interlock or overlap. One of the pros that I was playing with one day mentioned to me, "You've got to try and get a fit."

There's a crease in the lower part of your palm where the wrist and the hand come together. You've got to be able to have your thumb fit in there comfortably, because if it doesn't fit right, you wind up cutting the golf ball. You just don't have the proper grip on the club. To me, if I lose it a little bit right, it's because my grip is off.

Make sure your grip has the right fit

Everybody talks about the shaft being the most important thing in a golf club. I think the grip is the most important thing when it comes to swinging a club.

In the
Swing

Cheryl ANDERSON

Golf for Women *Magazine Top 50 Teacher*
Director of Instruction, Wykagyl Country Club,
New Rochelle, New York

Stretch your game.

As a golf instructor, the biggest factor I see in students not reaching their potential is their lack of strength and flexibility. Golfers today are mesmerized looking at videos of touring professionals' swings. They want their swings to look like the pros', but their bodies will not allow them to get into these same positions. Their bodies are not as strong or as flexible as most professional golfers'. Even the pros who don't look flexible, like Craig Stadler, or strong, like Corey Pavin, are much more athletic than they look.

Increase your strength and flexibility

I went through this same scenario years ago when I tried to change my swing and ended up with back, shoulder, and chest pains because my body was not very flexible or strong. A golf professional, Carl Rabito, advised me that instead of trying to just change my swing, I also needed to get into better shape by doing exercises tailored to the muscles used in the golf swing. At the time, there weren't many trainers focusing on golf, but I was fortunate to find one close to my home.

Since beginning this golf exercise program, I have significantly increased my range of motion and have strengthened my entire body, especially those muscles in my torso that create the stability necessary to generate powerful but controllable swings. I'm now pain free and have been able to develop the swing I have always wanted. If I had just worked on my swing, I never would have improved to anywhere near my current level.

$$\clubsuit$$

William C. BAKER

Chairman and CEO, Callaway Golf Company

About the only golf advice I rejected from Ely Callaway was given ten years ago when I joined the board of directors of Callaway Golf. Ely told me he would pay me a large sum of money to play and endorse golf clubs—so long as they were someone else's brand. Now, *there's* an endorsement. Ely was kidding, I think, but he knew the basic cause of my swing flaws as well as I do. I suffer from a loft problem. That's l-o-f-t, which in polite company is an acronym for "lack of fundamental talent." It has a slightly different translation in the locker room at Big Canyon Country Club in Newport Beach, California, where I sometimes play, but the meaning is the same.

However, since assuming the CEO position at my old friend Ely's company, I have had what amounts to a golf epiphany. I met the greatest golf teacher you have never heard of at the Callaway test center. His name is Randy Peterson, and he is one of these rare golf instructors who can fix elite tour pros and still help semidesperate cases like me. The lowest my handicap has ever been is 12. I'm an 18 right now, and depending on how long I can remember to do what Randy tells me, I may just get it down to 14. Like a lot of average golfers, my problem is that I hit a lot of weak shots to the right. Believe me, I had tried everything to cure this cursed slice, but it kept coming back. Nothing worked. That was until Randy got me to make a slight change in my backswing. Instead of fanning the club way open by what he calls "overrotating my arms," I now have a simple key Randy gave me. I focus on cocking my wrists, making sure I point the butt end of the club at the ball. This gets my swing on plane and makes it easier for me to square the club at impact, which leads to a hell of a lot more satisfying shots.

A good backswing can minimize your L.O.F.T.

Obviously, this hasn't cured my loft problem, but at least I can get the ball airborne most of the time.

Peggy Kirk BELL

LPGA Professional
World Golf Teachers Hall of Fame

When I started playing golf, I was blessed because I was taught by Leonard Schmutte, who was not only a great golf professional but also a fine player who traveled the PGA Tour with Horton Smith (who won the first Augusta Masters championship). Having been taught grip, posture, and alignment, I loved to hit balls on the range, just like so many other golfers. Leonard insisted that for every hour I spent hitting balls, I needed to spend equal time on my short game (putting, chipping, and pitching). If you have a good short game, your long game will improve.

Don't forget to waggle

Tommy Armour taught me how to waggle at address, which is the miniature golf swing. You must stay in motion, and you cannot think when you start your backswing. You must have a motion to tell your body to start the swing. Tommy taught me to start my backswing with a forward-press of the right knee. Today's players seem to forward press with their hands and arms, but they all have a motion of their own.

Pat BOONE

Singer

As a "celebrity" and an avid golfer since I was twenty years old, I've had the tremendous privilege of playing with some of the greats in all kinds of tournaments through the years. I'm talking about Arnold and Jack and Gary and Payne Stewart and Lee Elder and so many others.

Naturally, along the way, they've volunteered emergency advice for my erratic approaches, and in some cases I've actually asked for help, gratis, from the top pros along the way.

The best advice I ever received came from Doug Sanders, and I will now share it with you. Like most amateurs, I tend to sway off the ball, with disastrous or at least frustrating results. He stopped me once and said, "Look, Boone, when you start moving off the ball, put both feet together and take some practice swings. You'll find that if you sway at all, you'll fall over! Even in the middle of a round, you can do this a few times and even hit a couple of your shots with your feet totally together, and you'll find you'll get the ball inside out and on line, though not as far. Then transfer that same feeling of balance after you move your feet apart, and keep that feeling, okay?"

Be aware of balance

This from the pro who could take his backswing in a phone booth! But boy, it's helped me countless times.

Billy CASPER

More than Fifty PGA Tour Titles
Two-Time U.S. Open Champion
1970 Masters Champion
Five-Time Vardon Trophy Winner
Eight-Time Ryder Cup Team Member
World Golf Hall of Fame

I was playing in the 1956 Labatt Open in Quebec City, Canada. I was in the final group with Ted Kroll and we were on the twelfth fairway. He turned to me and said, "Billy, it appears you're going to win the tournament. Make certain you have a club in your hands to get the ball in the fairway because they're narrow."

I proceeded to birdie the fourteenth hole, and I was extremely excited to get to the fifteenth tee. There, I swung wildly and the ball ricocheted from tree to tree. I bogeyed that hole.

As we walked to the next tee, no words were spoken. Ted just nodded. I then remembered what he'd said on number twelve. So I kept the ball in the fairway the last three holes for my first PGA Tour win. From that point on, I reminded myself of Ted's advice and incorporated it into my game. It became a basic reason I was able to win fifty-one tour events.

Keep the ball in the fairway

My win at the 1959 U.S. Open at Winged Foot in Mamaroneck, New York, exemplified more than any other what Ted told me roughly three years prior. The third hole was about 210 yards, an uphill par 3 with a narrow green. It had a sand trap on the left and a grass bunker on the right. During the practice round, I decided that during all four rounds of the tournament, I would land the ball short of the trap at the front of the green with a five iron and chip onto the green. In four days, I made four pars that helped me toward a one-shot win over Bob Rosburg.

Well, Ted Kroll's advice proves that you can play more conservatively and still win no matter what club you use. You don't need to drive balls onto the greens.

Ted didn't have to help a young rookie like me. I will always have a great feeling for Ted Kroll.

Bobby CLAMPETT

Former PGA Tour Player
Analyst, CBS Sports

I was blessed to have had several very influential people in my golf career. Though it's difficult to come up with a single "best" golf tip, my first thought takes me back to when I was thirteen years old and taking golf lessons from Ben Doyle at my home course, the Carmel Valley Golf and Country Club. He explained to me the concept of "club-head lag," as explained in the book *The Golfing Machine*. After he showed me how to set the club at the top of the backswing by fully cocking the left wrist and setting the clubshaft on the number three pressure point (right index finger), I began hitting more solid golf shots, taking better divots with my irons in front of the ball, and hitting the ball farther. To further develop the feel, Ben had me do many practice drills in the long grass. The drill strengthened my wrists and helped me develop the proper feel through increased resistance caused from the club passing through the long grass. This clubhead lag became one of the trademarks of my swing and allowed me to be one of the longer hitters, pound for pound, on the PGA Tour.

Andrew W. CONWAY, Esq.

ProSports Management

The best golf advice I ever received was to practice hitting shots with no shoes on. Without the anchor of golf cleats, it is impossible to swing without maintaining proper balance. Once proper balance and tempo are achieved, putting your shoes back on will allow you to add power to the swing while maintaining proper balance.

Betsy CULLEN

LPGA Master Life Professional
Three LPGA Tour Titles
Golf Magazine *Top 50 Teacher*

Growing up in Oklahoma, "where the wind comes sweepin' down the plain," I always found it difficult to have any success playing golf in the wind.

It wasn't until I became a professional and was taking lessons from Harvey Penick on a windy day in Texas that I understood why. He casually made the comment during the lesson

Don't let bad weather rush you

that accidents, such as car wrecks, happen on windy days because the wind makes people excitable and easily rushed.

Several days after Harvey's lesson, I remembered that comment and put two and two together, realizing that I was swinging faster in the wind. I made an effort to slow down on those days the wind blew, and my game improved dramatically. I couldn't believe how insightful Harvey had been and how subtle his approach was.

Michael DOUGLAS

Actor

My two worst tendencies are tempo and coming over the top. I have found over the years that two early pieces of advice still hold true. To control your tempo, say "Cindy Crawford" very quietly to yourself as you begin your backswing. And don't even think of starting to come down until you finish the "ford" part. Obviously, I have changed the name since my marriage, and I must say Catherine's full name works very well, too.

As far as coming over the top, aiming your club for one o'clock on the through swing tends to eliminate a lot of shanks and slices. I stick a tee in the ground at one o'clock to give me a visual line and put a string along the twelve o'clock line.

Nick FALDO

Three-Time British Open Champion
Three-Time Masters Champion
Eleven-Time Ryder Cup Team Member
World Golf Hall of Fame

The best piece of advice ever given to me was by my first coach, Ian Connelly, more than thirty years ago. His advice was the importance of getting your tempo right, and it has stood the test of time.

Whether you hit the ball slowly, soft, or hard, everyone needs tempo. With it, you should be able to drive the ball smoother and the same distance with a seven iron as you can with a six and a five iron. Tempo is the glue that sticks all elements of the golf swing together.

> **Imitate a good player's tempo**

My advice to anyone looking to improve his or her game is to pick a player whose swing he or she admires and then try to emulate that player, copying his or her tempo.

Jim FAZIO

Architect (designed Trump National Golf Club, Westchester, New York, and Trump International Golf Club, Palm Beach, Florida)

George Fazio was a touring professional in the late 1940s and early 1950s. He tied for the U.S. Open in 1950 with Ben Hogan and Lloyd Mangrum at Merion Golf Club in Philadelphia. It was one of his home courses . . . I guess you could say he was a pretty good player in his day. He did lose in the play-off, though.

I didn't really know my uncle until I was about fifteen

years old. He was a golf pro somewhere, and I was always playing baseball. I went to work for him that summer doing maintenance on a golf course he owned. During that time at the course, I started playing. I was a left-handed baseball player trying to play golf right-handed . . . it wasn't pretty. He gave me one lesson the entire time I was around him, from 1957 to 1986—he changed my grip, and that was it.

Learn to hold your backswing

But he did say two things, and he said them many times. The first was if you could hold your backswing, you could teach yourself—the point being how and where the club passed the ball to get to where it is now.

The second was when he was on the tour. Back then, there were a lot of characters on the tour, and they all traveled from tournament to tournament by car. After a round of golf, they'd sit around and talk. One day, they were trying to describe the golf swing in the fewest words possible. My uncle's definition of the golf swing was *more through and less to.*

Bruce FLEISHER

Seventeen Champions Tour Titles

Flexibility becomes a greater issue with age. Consequently, more time must be spent practicing turning during the golf swing. We all get older, and to keep our games at their peak, turning back enough in the swing becomes an issue. How far is enough?

I've solved that problem by letting my left shoulder control the length of my backswing. My only through swing is turning back far enough for the left shoulder to point behind the ball. Without my having to think about anything else, my hands and arms swing automatically up and over my shoulders at the top of the backswing.

> **Turn your shoulder behind the ball**

If more people could just turn their shoulder behind the ball, they would not have to concern themselves with twenty other swing thoughts like weight shift, swing plane, and so on. Simply turning the shoulder easily lengthens the swing arc.

James A. FRANK

Editor in Chief, Golf Connoisseur

Like Mr. Trump, I'm a native New Yorker. Well, not exactly. I'm really from New Jersey, but very close to New York City, close enough that beginning with summer jobs and then for more than twenty-five years of my professional life, I commuted daily from the leafy suburbs to the concrete canyons.

Inevitably, the city rubbed off on me, and I picked up more than a bit of the Big Apple's famously fast pace.

For the last twenty years, I've been in the golf business, as editor of *Golf Magazine* for eighteen-plus years and now heading up a new, upscale lifestyle magazine called *Golf Connoisseur.* As part of my job, I've traveled to those parts of the country where golf is played year-round and golf equipment is made—places like the Deep South, Phoenix, and Southern California—and more than once the locals remarked that I obviously was a New Yorker, because I was moving more quickly than what they were used to. I describe it as "running at seventy-eight in a thirty-three world" (for those of you who remember the phonograph). In meetings and at sales conferences and trade shows, moving at a New York pace usually proved very effective. Where it didn't work was on the golf course.

In 1989, I began working with Dave Pelz, the short-game guru who was a *Golf Magazine* teaching editor and remains one of the most creative thinkers in the game (as well as a truly nice man). I would help Dave write his monthly instruction articles, which meant we'd have to get together three or four times a year to discuss stories and photograph them. That would mean leaving Gotham for wherever Dave happened to be leading one of his golf schools, working with his tour pro students, or taking a well-earned rest between teaching gigs. I'd always try to make the trips when it was cold back East, and we would meet at one of his schools—in Palm Springs, Boca Raton, or another warm golf spot—near that week's PGA Tour stop, or at his home in Austin, Texas. (And if we had to work during the summer, we'd go to Vail.) Tough duty, indeed. And, not surprisingly, we'd often find a way to sneak a round or two into the schedule.

It was early in our working relationship that Dave said to me, after playing a few holes together, that my surefire inconsistency was attributable to something he labeled "the New York hit." I wasn't swinging the club; I was trying to hit the ball, and moving much too fast as a result. He'd seen this condition many times before in his amateur students, especially the ones from back East and those who took their work too seriously. I took little comfort in the fact that I was a victim of both geography and job.

Avoid the "New York hit"

But there was hope. I was already learning the Pelz method and seeing great improvement within one hundred yards of the green. One of the tenets of Dave's teaching is a full, flowing, rhythmic swing, which is absolutely vital to a good short game (if you don't believe me, watch any tour pro and you'll see what I mean). So I was capable of making a swing, not a hit. At least with a wedge.

Changing my long game wasn't as easy, and still isn't. In fact, more than fifteen years after first working with Pelz—we've written hundreds of articles and three bestselling books, including his short-game and putting "bibles"—I still have to think about the "New York hit," and not doing it. Sometimes I think about swinging the club rather than hitting the ball, other times about slowing my tempo (at least on the backswing, which has been described more than once as happening at blinding speed). I try to envision the silky motions of Sam Snead and Ernie Els. I even tell myself to pretend to be swinging a wedge, although I'm holding a driver.

Some days I succeed; others, I surely don't. But I've seen it work. And there isn't a round in which I don't think to myself, at least a dozen times, "Tempo, tempo, tempo."

Swinging (rather than hitting) on every shot is my ultimate goal, and I intend to reach it someday. Such patience is possible, but first I'll have to exorcise another demon—nearly thirty years of battling New York City traffic.

Sophie GUSTAFSON

Four LPGA Tour Titles
Four-Time Solheim Cup Team Member

Ever since I was a little girl learning to play golf with my older brother Pär, I wanted to hit the ball long—really long. I didn't want to hit "like a girl" or be looked at as less powerful. I learned that whenever I wanted to really rip at the ball, I should take a little wider stance than normal. To be able to hit the ball up in the air, I also put the ball a little bit further up in my stance. You do a few wiggles with your arms and wrists so that you feel that you are as relaxed as you can possibly be (for hitting a three-hundred-yard drive!). Then, feel like you are taking your club back in a wide path . . . feel like your hands are traveling a little further out from your body than normal. The key to hitting a real long drive is to make sure that you finish your backswing before you start your downswing. A lot of amateurs are in such a hurry when they are trying to hit it far that they never finish their backswing. When that happens, your whole body gets out of sync, and you are bound to hit it off the map. So when you get to the top and you are sure that your backswing is finished, just rip at it as hard as you can. That is what I always do, and now my brother has to work pretty hard to keep up with me.

Penny HARDAWAY

New York Knicks

The best golf advice I have gotten and that I follow to this day is pretty simple—stand connected and take the swing as one piece from the top of your body all the way through. The more consistently you can do that, the more you will enjoy playing. It is something that makes each time I play more enjoyable.

Mike KEISER

Owner, Bandon Dunes Golf Resort
Cofounder, Recycled Paper Greetings, Inc.

I just recently got the best golf advice I have ever received. It was from Kevin Costello, a 6 handicap from Shinnecock and the Greens Committee chairman. I get steadily worse when I play with him. We were playing at Barnbougle Dunes in Tasmania and I was getting really bad, and Kevin couldn't help himself. After I topped two balls on a par 3, he said to me, "I can't take it anymore. I just have to give you a lesson."

Bend from the knees

So we finished the hole, and on the next tee he said, "It's your posture." He showed me I was bending over too much from tension. "Don't bend from the back but at the knees," he said. He made me use my knees as a hinge and maintain the posture I used with my driver. I realized that the shorter the club in my hand, the more I had been leaning over.

I tried what he said and it felt foreign for a couple of holes, but, within two or three holes, my swing became much easier and I was hitting at the pin. I'm convinced it was the best lesson I've ever gotten.

Peter KESSLER

Columnist, Golf Magazine
President, The Perfect Club Company

I have hosted more than six hundred live, one-hour television shows on golf instruction with more than three hundred of the finest teachers, including the instructors on everyone's shortest list of the best in the game.

I have listened to more than fifty thousand tips from these one-hour programs, and I have learned three important things about playing golf.

1. You can't think your way through the golf swing.

2. If you must think of one swing key that's mechanical, make it apply to the forward swing rather than the backswing.

3. The most reliable swing key, if you must have one, is to always strive to swing the club at what you know to be your most successful rhythm.

Don't overthink the golf swing

William LAUDER

President and CEO, Estée Lauder

Don't be rigid. Be flexible as your stroke changes and make sure to keep your weight back until you make contact with the ball. Enjoy yourself on the golf course and, most important, play for fun. The best games always come when you're not keeping score.

Bruce LIETZKE

Thirteen PGA Tour Titles
Seven Champions Tour Titles

This is my thirtieth year of using the exact same swing. I wasn't told to do that thirty years ago. I wasn't told that this is the swing you are going to be able to play with the rest of your life. But it's a swing that evolved in the minitours.

In those days, I shaped the ball in most directions. I had swings for hooks and fades and all that. I played the minitours in 1974, and I got down to Florida when the wind was blowing really hard and I didn't know how to hit a real low shot. Somewhere in those minitour adventures, trying to learn to play in the Florida wind, I developed this swing where I came over the ball a little bit and every shot produced a fade. I really became kind of distressed about it because I couldn't hit a hook when I wanted.

My oldest brother, Duane, had been and still is to this day the only teacher I ever worked with. I called him from Florida and told him something had happened to my swing and that all I could do was fade the ball. I just couldn't hook anything, and he needed to get down here—he lived in Oklahoma—and straighten out my swing.

He was a golf salesman and couldn't get away. In the meantime, I won a whole bunch of money on the mini-tours with that new swing. Then I actually made it through a tour qualifying school, and that's when I probably got the best advice of my life. I'd been calling Duane and complaining about my swing, and he'd say, "What did you shoot today?"

I'd say, "I hit a sixty-five, but I hate this swing and I can't hit a hook." Then he spoke the words I've lived by ever since. He said, "Well, just stick with that swing until it breaks down. Then we can get together and I'll figure out what you're doing wrong. In the meantime, you just made it to the tour. Now is not the time to start making changes. You just need to play this thing out. Finish your first year on the tour with this swing, and in the off-season we'll try to find the problem."

We had no video cameras back then. So I didn't have any film I could send to him. His advice was "Let's stick with this swing until it fails, then we'll go to work and fix it."

That was thirty years ago, and I have never changed one thing in any part of my golf swing, not my grip or my stance or the length of my clubs. I haven't gone to longer or lighter clubs. They are exactly the same as they were thirty years ago. I've tried to keep my equipment the same, and that helped me maintain that same swing. I think this applies a lot to amateur golfers. There are not many guys who haven't done a lot of experimenting. Freddie Couples hasn't messed with his swing, and I've talked with Jack Nicklaus enough to know that he has never really changed his swing.

Stick with a swing that works

I'm probably at one end of the spectrum, and then there are the other guys, who are constantly practicing new swings or new techniques or trying out new equipment all the time. That's what the amateur kind of falls into. He will buy a radically long driver, a forty-eight-inch driver, and that changes that muscle memory he had developed from a regular driver. It's gone.

They go to a teacher, and he's telling them what the new Tiger Woods wisdom is. I think the amateurs should just try to find that one swing they're comfortable with and stay with it. There is nothing wrong with going out and trying to be a little bit better. But you don't want to lose the swing that you have. That's probably the biggest fear of any pro golfer, that they'll lose it. Like an Ian Baker-Finch or Chip Beck or David Duval. They changed things and totally lost what they had to begin with. A lot of guys have been great players and won tournaments, but they continued to tinker. Low-ball hitters wanted to hit it high, or high-ball hitters wanted to hit it low, and they gave up the swing they had and they came crashing down.

It took me two or three years to decide that my swing wasn't going to break down. I had to test it under pressure. It also fit my lifestyle of wanting to come home and not touch a golf club for a couple weeks. I've never been addicted to practicing golf. My course in Beaumont, Texas, didn't have a driving range, so I never learned to practice golf at all. Having that one swing to go back to was a lot easier when I took a couple of weeks off.

Mike McGETRICK

Owner, McGetrick Golf Academy
Number 8, Golf Digest's America's 50 Greatest Teachers
(teaches several top PGA and LPGA players)

Don't fix your swing for eighteen holes. You must learn to play *golf,* not *golf swing.*

In order to let the champion in you emerge, you need to adopt the proper mind-set when you're on the course. So many golfers tinker with their swing for eighteen holes because they think that good shots will only be born out of perfect technique. When you tinker with your swing for an entire round of golf, not only will your performance suffer, but you can tinker yourself right out of some good fundamentals. When you get wrapped up in swing fundamentals on the course, you're not playing *golf,* you're playing *golf swing.*

If you ask top professionals how many shots they hit in a round of golf that were hit absolutely perfectly, they'll tell you it was probably only a handful, even though they may have scored very well. The difference between the top player's approach and the average golfer's is that the top player knows how to produce an A score on a day when he or she doesn't have his or her A swing. The next time you warm up on the range before you play, note how well you're swinging that day. You may not have your best stuff (i.e., your A swing), and in fact you may have your B or even C swing. In any case, it's important to take whatever swing you have that day to the course. If you've got a little fade going on the range before the round, aim a little more to the left and use one more club than you normally would for shots during the round, then head to the range after playing to work on the particulars of your setup or swing. Your task for the round is to shoot an A score with your B or C swing—then you're really playing *golf.*

Focus on the game, not the swing

Patti McGOWAN

Golf Magazine *Top 100 Teacher*

This is a tip both for hitting the ball, as well as to create a good mind-set for playing the game. It is vastly different from the way people have been traditionally taught.

At the setup, make sure you are firmly and athletically braced up from the ground and behind the ball. Then, within the framework of your own feet, just take the club back short and hit the ball really hard.

Several years ago, everyone would take the club back really long, and we were all taught to drive our legs. Unfortunately, what happened was the legs would get way in front and basically beat the arms and the golf club to the ball. It not only caused a lack of power, but it is really bad on the back. These days, you see everyone hitting the ball so much farther. Why? Because they're standing firmly braced to the ground. Since they're taking the club back so much shorter, braced from the beginning, they can swing a lot harder and hit the ball harder because the arms and the club arrive at the ball with the body. The body hasn't beaten the golf club to the ball.

Brace yourself

This also helps create a much more assertive, "no-fear" mentality. Without so many things to worry about, the swing is much more simple and powerful. When I was growing up, it was all about finessing everything—taking it back really far and swinging really slow. But if you have to swing really slow, there's a problem. You shouldn't have to swing slow in order to hit the ball.

John MAHAFFEY

Ten PGA Tour Titles
Champions Tour Player

The best advice I ever received came from the legendary Ben Hogan. While I was playing practice rounds with Mr. Hogan for the 1970 Colonial Invitational in Fort Worth, Texas, he stressed how important alignment was for consistent shotmaking. Mr. Hogan told me, "John, you are going to find out that when your game is not as sharp as it should be, it will almost always be a result of poor alignment. It is the most important element in your preshot routine."

Visualize during alignment

Mr. Hogan took me aside and showed me the proper position at address.

"You must visualize two parallel lines," he told me. "The first is the line to the hole—your target. The second is the line directly in front of your feet allowing you to align your feet, hips, and shoulders parallel to your target line." He continued, "Your right foot has to be perpendicular to both parallel lines. Your left foot has to be turned out slightly toward your target. The reason for positioning your feet this way is to allow you to create a coiling on the backswing and a full release on the downswing."

In all of the video footage of Mr. Hogan, you will always see him in this position.

Bill MORETTI

President and Owner, Academy of Golf Dynamics

To get results on the course, practice your finish.

Work on a proper finish for 50 percent of your practice time. Most golf instruction is written for the setup and the backswing, and a little for the downswing.

Little, if any, is written on the finish. Some amateurs do have some success with backswing thoughts on the range, but only a small percentage hit the ball with the same success on the course as they do on the range. When golfers have to deal with rough, out-of-bounds markers, hazards, bets, tournaments, or scoring pressure, they freeze up with their swings because they are nervous and unfamiliar with the finish.

> **Spend more time on achieving a proper finish**

If amateurs knew the proper finish and worked on it for 50 percent of their practice time instead of 100 percent on backswing thoughts, the results they would get on the practice range would be the same as the course.

For a proper finish, the shoulders are on top of the hips and the arms are in front of the body.

For a slice finish, the shoulders finish around and in front of the hips. The arms are swung very flat.

For a hook finish, the shoulders finish under and over the right leg. The arms are swung very upright.

When practicing the finish, set the club at address eight inches behind where the ball would be. From this position, swing into the finish position with no backswing—just swing into the correct finish position.

Do this drill, then make a full golf swing and try to get into the same correct finish position. Practice the finish and the backswing for equal amounts of time and you will hit shots better on the course. Remember that 50 percent of the swing is the *finish*.

Jerry MOWLDS

Golf Magazine *Top 100 Teacher*

My best tip was accidental.

When playing with a senior pro when I was a young assistant, I noticed that he drove his ball exactly the same every time: a slight left to right fade that started out left center and ended up right center. It was so impressive that I began to watch closely. He had his driver hooded (closed) at address, a rather strong grip (turned to the right with both hands), and a quite closed stance! Finally, after about twelve perfect drives, I asked him how he hit that perfect fade every time with a setup like that. He then gave me the secret of golf. He replied, "Oh, that damned slice; I've been trying to get rid of that shot for thirty years!" I then remembered that as a

Ball flight patterns are backward

caddy, my steady loop was quite a gambler, and he had a hook. I also remember that every time he overhooked, he started out with the clubface "opened out" at address and swinging to the right.

It's all backward! That day has helped my own game immensely for the past forty years, as well as countless clients whom I have helped to understand ball flight.

Larry NELSON

1983 U.S. Open Champion
Two PGA Tour Titles

Burt Seagraves once told me that shots do not lie. The direction the club moves and the way the face is positioned at impact dictates where the ball goes and how it gets there. So I developed my swing, very simply, around this concept, and I am able to fix any problem in my swing quickly.

David OGRIN

1996 La Cantera Texas Open Champion

Over the course of my twenty-plus years on the PGA Tour, I have received a lot of advice on golf. But the very best is the advice I've paid for.

Dr. Jim Suttie, who teaches in Illinois and Florida, saved my career in 1991. I was in a terrible slump, and was hitting shots I called "scuds." I would often launch a scud into somebody's backyard. This is *not* good for a pro golfer. It took Doc and me six sessions—not just one-hour lessons but all-day marathons— to get me fixed. It was hard work, but these are the two key things I learned.

Use video to study your swing

First, the proper use of video absolutely works in helping a player improve his golf swing. Doc would film me and then compare me side by side with other great players. What I discovered was that the other guys all had positions in common and I was different. They were making money and I was missing cuts. I needed to change. I did, but I did it by using video properly—and, in my opinion, nobody in this country uses video better than Jim Suttie.

Second, everybody swings differently based on body type and other factors. Doc showed me what makes me swing the club well and why what others do would not work for me. We would have discussions in the evening as to why Ray Floyd and Jack Nicklaus were both great, yet those two swings were miles apart. From Suttie, I learned that my swing was good enough to compete on the tour. This teaching in 1991 was the foundation for my win in 1996.

I also want to share the one thing I always tell my pro-am partners. Eventually, I will ask one of my amateurs to step out and take some practice swings. Inevitably, those practice swings are free, easy, and full. Only in true beginners do I ever see a bad swing. When I show all the players in the group how well the man out front is swinging, I tell them this: "If you want to practice your swing, you can do that in the office. If you want to improve your swing, do it without a ball. The problems start when we introduce the ball. Now you switch from swinging the club to hitting the ball. These are two different things. The key is as simple as this: hit the ball with the same swing you have when you take a practice swing."

Jerry PATE

Eight PGA Tour Titles
1976 U.S. Open Champion
Champions Tour Player

Without a doubt, the best golf advice I ever received was from my father. He gave me the opportunity to start golf when I was six. One statement he always drilled into my head, even to the day he passed away at age sixty-nine, was tempo, tempo, tempo. He always taught me that no matter what type of biomechanical flaws you might have in your golf swing, with precise timing the clubhead can return squarely to the ball in a repetitive manner. I will always value this lesson from my dad as a foundation for my success in this great game.

George PEPER

Executive Editor, Links *Magazine*

After forty years of playing golf, I got my best tip in 2004. The source was my old buddy (and USGA executive director) David Fay. We were on the eighteenth hole of the Casa de Campo resort in the Dominican Republic and all morning long he'd been watching me flail haplessly at my iron shots, cutting violently across the ball, producing enormous leftward-pointing divots and pitifully weak fades. (Come to think of it, Fay had been watching me flail haplessly for about three decades, without saying a word! Why he picked this particular day to speak up, I'll never know—probably, having won some of my money that morning, he was feeling magnanimous. But I'm very glad he did.)

Pretend the ball is on the center of a clockface

"Yank the clubhead back way inside on your takeaway," he said. "Pretend the ball's sitting on the center of a clockface, and take your club back toward four or even five o'clock. It'll probably feel strange to you, but just do it, because right now your backswing has more detours than Jim Furyk's."

I tried it, struck a nine iron to ten feet, and have never looked back. No more slashing, no more beaver pelts, no more left-to-right powder-puff shots—just piercing draws. Thank goodness, too, because I've moved to St. Andrews, and on these windy, gorse-lined links there's no sympathy for a weak fade.

Don POOLEY

Two PGA Tour Titles
2002 U.S. Senior Open Champion
Champions Tour Player

I have had countless lessons in my thirty-year professional career, but the best tip I ever received was from Larry Nelson in 1977. Larry has had a fabulous career on tour, winning three major championships and many other tournaments on both the PGA Tour and the Champions Tour.

I have a great respect for Larry's knowledge of the golf swing. In 1977, I was struggling with my swing when Larry offered this advice. He told me that all players with good swings kept their right leg (for right-handers) at the same angle throughout the backswing. If you break that plane to the right, it is a sway. If you break that plane to the left, it is a reverse pivot. Both faults create serious problems for consistency.

I had a sway in my swing at that time. So, to correct this fault, I had to turn my right leg around to prevent that drift to the right. My swing became more repeatable almost immediately. The shots were straighter and more solid!

Check your leg angle

Since that lesson twenty-eight years ago, I periodically check my right-leg angle in the backswing. It is a fundamental part of the golf swing, and if you do it, your shots will become more consistent, too.

Brad REDDING

PGA Master Professional
Golf Magazine *Top 100 Teacher*

Most golfers have been told that the first move in the downswing is a turning of the hips. One of the best ball strikers of all time, Ben Hogan, popularized this in his book *Five Lessons: The Modern Fundamentals of Golf.* Most golfers, however, do not know that a sweeping hook plagued Mr. Hogan early in his career. Because of this, he was able to clear his hips out of the way in the downswing. This move helped him to control his hook, and in fact allowed him to hit a controlled fade. Eighty to ninety percent of the golfing population tends to slice the ball. This "modern-day" tip is of no use to them.

To understand the downswing, you need to know that the golf swing is a system that works on three areas: the body, the hands, and the clubhead. Each area moves different directions and, as a result, at different speeds.

The button on your shirt placket is your body. It moves 4 to 5 inches in the entire swing and 1 to 2 miles per hour. The hands move 5-6 feet in the golf swing and 4 to 5 miles per hour. The clubhead moves about 16 to 20 feet in the golf swing and 60 to 120 miles per hour. So all these areas are moving different distances and at different speeds, but they all need to move at the same rate of rotation. They must be in sync.

Many golfers believe that in order to hit the ball farther, they need to turn their hips faster. This leads to the body outracing the hands and the club-head. The clubface cannot close, so they slice the ball. To get your swing in sync and to turn all those slices into straight shots—or better yet, draws—you need to get the hands and the clubhead to move at the same rate as the body.

Don't let your body outrace the clubhead

Take the club to the top of your backswing. From here, do not turn your hips or your shoulders, and let your arms drop straight down. Your right hand will separate from your right shoulder. The distance the hands are from the right shoulder should increase, your right arm will begin to straighten, and your forearms and hands will begin to close the clubface. Notice how little your body has turned compared to how much farther your arms and hands have moved. This allows the arms to drop and gets them in front of the body and not "trapped" behind it. As your hands continue to separate from your right shoulder, continue to turn your forearms and hands over so that the clubface is closing. As you reach impact, the toe will be closer to the ball than the heel. It will be as if you are hitting the ball with the toe of the club.

Your shoulders have turned, but only because your arms have moved. Your hips have turned, but only as a function to get the clubhead to impact. Do this drill slowly at first until you can do it smoothly and in sync. Then try it with some tees. After that, try it with the ball teed up. Don't be surprised if the ball does not hook. It only takes a tenth of a second for the club to move from the top of your backswing to impact. That isn't a lot of time, so you need to start the turning of the clubface sooner than you think.

Jimmy ROBERTS

Commentator, NBC Sports

I think everybody has gotten a million pieces of advice regarding golf, but there are two that stick out in my mind.

The first one comes from the man whom I consider to be the greatest golf instructor of our time, Jim Flick. Among others, he has taught Jack Nicklaus and Tom Lehman. The list goes on and on and on, but you don't need to take that list any further than just Jack Nicklaus.

Jim told me that he thought one of the problems with golf instruction was that people got paralysis by analysis. They would have too many thoughts in their head and would try to do too much.

He gave me one tip, which I have always found very, very useful. He said that when you're swinging the club, you should try to feel the weight of the clubhead, especially on the backswing. He said that would deal with several different issues. If you feel the weight of the clubhead, you can't grip the club too tightly. If you feel the weight of the clubhead, you can't swing the club too fast. So it corrects a number of evils, probably a bunch that I don't even realize. It always worked for me. That was number one.

Avoid paralysis by analysis

The second one came from a show I used to do for ESPN called *Golf's Greatest Legends*. It involved going around the country talking to some of the game's great players. I asked Greg Norman, "What's the one tip that you would give the average golfer?" He said that the one thing he sees the average golfer do way too often is not take enough club. So his one piece of advice was not to let your ego get in the way—make sure that you take enough club because, more times than not, average golfers tend to go by some book or make some determination of how far they should hit each club rather than how they actually do hit each club.

Doug SANDERS

Twenty PGA Tour Titles

When I was a young man, I was told by my golf professional, Maurice Hudson, in Cedartown, Georgia, to "always take plenty of club and swing slow and easy."

Of all the pro-ams I have played in my life, I have very seldom seen a good shot hit over the pin on a fly by an amateur. They always think they can hit it farther than they actually can. The amateurs look for the ball in the rough, and it is never found while walking toward the green. It is almost always found by someone from behind, at a much shorter distance than they thought it was. That, again, is an indication that you think you can hit it longer than you actually can. It is difficult even for a pro to hit the ball solid every time by hitting it real hard. So it is almost impossible for an amateur to swing very hard and be accurate. If you want your game to improve, take plenty of club and swing slow and easy where you can catch it solid and be consistent. I know I did not win twenty PGA professional championships by swinging hard and hitting as far as I could each time; I was smarter than that. This is the reason I was a winner—and, by taking this advice, you can be, too.

Take plenty of club

Scott SEIFFERLEIN

*PGA Instructor, Middle Bay Country Club,
Oceanside, New York*

So many golfers are advised that their poor shots are a result of "lifting their head." This is almost always *not* the case. If you have been repeatedly told that you are lifting your head, you will make such a conscious, unnatural effort to keep your head down that you will never be able to react to the natural weight transfer of the golf swing. This will result in poor contact and a lack of distance. I have videotaped hundreds of golfers who have been told that they are lifting their head. Time after time the high-speed, frame-by-frame video clearly shows that they are keeping their head down long after impact.

Phil SIMMS

New York Giants, 1979–1993

I have a compulsive personality. I played in the New Jersey State Amateur Tournament about six times. I would stay out on the course so long that I was getting back spasms the two days before the tournament.

I played in a celebrity golf tournament in Lake Tahoe during a time when I was playing quite a bit of golf and thought I was a good player. You know the nerves. I teed off of the very first hole and hit it right down the middle, a beautiful drive. I hit a pitching wedge to about fifteen feet of the hole on the green. I went up and, for the first time in my life, went cross-handed putting. I never practiced it, really, nothing. But for some reason, as I was getting ready to putt, I thought, "This cross-handed thing looks pretty good." I used it and made the putt and I thought, "Man, this game is just unbelievable." It would be like all of a sudden lining up behind the center and throwing the ball left-handed.

Take lessons to hit farther

The best advice I can say about the golf course for me is this: I have played golf with some wonderful businesspeople in New Jersey, and I would say I have been given ten great pieces of business advice on the golf course and nine of them turned out to be home runs. The sad part of it is that I didn't act on a single one of them. They say golf is great for business. You know what? It could have been.

I didn't take a lot of lessons, but I played in a lot of tournaments. For my compulsive personality, golf is quite something. That's the best way to say it. If putting for twenty minutes helps your game, then putting for five hours straight can really help your game.

I have taken many typical lessons over the years and gotten lots of technical advice. What golfer doesn't? I'll never forget a pro who gave me a lot of lessons. His name is Ed Whitman. He plays on the Senior Tour here and there and is very well known. I think he is by far the most accomplished golfer among local pros in the history of the Tristate area. We had been working together quite a bit.

One day he said to me, "What are you actually trying to do by taking all these lessons?" He knew I was a pretty good player and all that stuff.

I said, "Well, what do you mean? There's only one reason why I'd take a lesson. So I can swing harder and hit it farther." Ed laughed and said, "Well, of course." He loved it. That was exactly what he wanted to hear. Why else would you play golf? Man, you want to hit that thing as hard as you can.

Being a quarterback in the NFL, I only had one agenda. Listen, they can talk about putting and all that other stuff about the game. There is nothing like standing on the tee and just hitting it as hard as you can hit it. It's the best.

Ozzie SMITH

National Baseball Hall of Fame

The best advice was being told I should always try to use the instincts I was blessed with.

To best be able to use those instincts, you should make sure before you get started that you have your hands lined up properly, that you have a good feel, a good grip on the golf club, and that your body is in the right position to fire properly.

It's about not swinging too hard, allowing the club to do the work. That's probably the most important thing. We have a tendency sometimes to want to try and lift the ball.

It should do what the club was built to make it do. You just learn to allow the club to do what it's supposed to do and not overswing because the ball is sitting still. When you overswing, you have a tendency to get to the outside of the ball and end up hooking it.

Allow the club to do the work

John SMOLTZ

Atlanta Braves

If somebody gives me advice and I feel it right away and it works, it's great advice. And if I don't feel it, it's never gonna work. So the best advice I was given was simply that if I want to fade a ball, I should finish my swing higher. And if I want to hook a ball, I should finish lower with my arms.

So, if my arms stayed below my shoulders, I was drawing a ball. And if I finished above my shoulders with my arms, I was fading a ball. And that really has been the easiest transition in trying to do something with my golf swing.

Kellie STENZEL

Golf for Women *Magazine Top 50 Teacher
Author,* The Women's Guide to Golf: A Handbook
for Beginners, The Women's Guide to Consistent
Golf, *and* The Women's Guide to Lower Scores

I divide the best golf advice I ever received into two parts: the advice when I was playing and the advice since I started teaching.

The best golf advice I received when I was playing was from my father, Bob Stenzel, who played on the PGA Tour. His advice was "Miss it straight and have a good short game." I always built this goal into my practice. If I did not hit a good shot and it went straight, I trained myself to let it go and be content with the fact that more often than not it was still in play. And by focusing a lot of my practice time on my short game, I could often get this straight miss close enough to the hole to one putt and recover.

**Fix the setup to
fix the swing**

The best golf advice I received since I have been teaching was from Mike Adams, whom I taught with for three years at PGA National in Palm Beach Gardens, Florida. His advice was "Fix the setup and the swing will take care of itself." Requiring each student to have a good grip, good posture, good ball position, and good alignment made it so much easier to produce a good golf swing. The proper grip helps to produce a square clubface at impact and allows security without tension, helping to generate speed as well as allowing the wrists to hinge properly. Proper posture provides balance, which helps to produce solid contact. Proper ball position allows the body to stack in an athletic position and helps to deliver square impact to the golf ball. Good alignment allows the golfer to make the proper swing without having to compensate otherwise to get the golf ball back to the target.

I have been endlessly amazed at the results I get from my students by following this advice from Mike. Many times I have suggested they correct their setup—either the grip, the ball position, the posture, or the alignment—and without any further advice their golf swing gets instantly better. This makes teaching a lot of fun.

Cary STEPHAN

Head Professional, Trump National Golf Club,
Westchester, New York

Being the head professional at Trump National Golf Club in Westchester, New York, has been a terrific experience, one that's surpassed my wildest dreams. The facility is second to none, with more than two hundred acres of pure golf heaven all within a thirty-minute drive from Midtown Manhattan. The membership roster is a who's who of movie stars, sporting legends, and Fortune 500 CEOs.

I have compiled what I feel to be some of the most important elements of a sound golf swing. These are, in my opinion, common in most proficient swings. Give these a try and remember, "Rome was not built in a day." Golf is a most difficult game.

THE GRIP: Keep your left hand in a strong position (able to see three knuckles as you look down from address). Keep your right hand in a neutral position (palm facing target line). *Tip: Hold the club as lightly as you must throughout the entire swing.*

THE STANCE: The longer the club you are using, the wider the stance you should take. Get athletic and flex your knees a bit. *Tip: The right shoulder is lower than the left, the right hip is lower than the left, and the right knee is lower than the left.*

THE TAKEAWAY: The shoulders, arms, and hands all move in unity. Turn your left shoulder under your chin and try to stretch it behind (to the right of) the ball. Allow the wrists to hinge on their own relatively late in the backswing. *Tip: "Feel" the weight of the club-head throughout the backswing by maintaining the constant light grip pressure.*

A great golf game is not built in a day

THE TRANSITION: Take time to reflect. A slight pause from the completion of the backswing to the start of the downswing allows for the proper sequence of movements critical to solid contact. These movements begin with the weight being returned to the left leg and allowing the arms to "fall" slightly before the unwinding of the shoulders. *Tip: Maintain constant light grip pressure and relaxed wrists in transition to store power and keep the club on plane.*

IMPACT: This is the moment of truth. The body's rotation is critical here. Most of the weight should be shifted to the left foot and the hips and torso are rotating quickly, pulling the shoulders, arms, and club with tremendous force. There are no conscious thoughts of clubface position or what the hands are doing; they are along for the ride. *Tip: Maintaining light grip pressure through impact eliminates "clutching" and allows for the club to swing its fastest with the least amount of effort.*

FOLLOW THROUGH: Let it go! The body continues its rotation until 99 percent of the weight is transferred to the front foot and the arms and club shaft have straightened out while you keep the head over the right side of the body. This is a full release of all the power stored up during the swing. Again, no conscious effort to release the wrists is needed—they will on their own. *Tip: Keep the clubhead traveling level to the ground as long as possible after impact to increase accuracy and distance.*

FINISH POSITION: You're not home yet. If there is one thing in all my years of teaching that I feel is most underrated, it would be the importance of the finish position. I have yet to see one single tournament golfer have success falling backward as he or she hits the ball! However, my lesson book is filled with those who have mastered that move. Unfortunately, it's a rather basic concept, and many don't want to spend time working on it. Get your weight to the front foot and leg. Finish with your right shoulder closer to the target than your left. Have your belt buckle facing left of the target. Your right toe is the only part of your foot touching the ground. *Tip: Hold the finish position in balance until the ball hits the ground.*

Mike TURNESA Jr.

Head Pro Instructor, Rockville Links Country Club, Long Island, New York

Growing up with what has been referred to as "golf's first family," the seven Turnesa brothers, I received more advice about the game than one could absorb in several lifetimes.

My dad, Mike Sr., lost in the finals of the 1948 PGA Championship to Ben Hogan; my uncle Jim won the 1952 PGA Championship; Uncle Joe was runner-up to Bobby Jones in the 1926 U.S. Open and Walter Hagen in the 1927 PGA; and Uncle Willie, known as "Willie the Wedge" and the only Turnesa not to turn professional, won the U.S. Amateur at Oakmont and the British Amateur in 1938.

Tempo is the key

And while I was the recipient of all this golf advice, the most important lessons I learned from my family were to always be a gentleman on and off the course and remember that tempo is the key to a great golf swing. You may have thought that my dad and uncles, being self-taught, would have had unorthodox swings; but no, every one of them was very smooth, right on top of the ball, with no hang-back—textbook!

Daniel C. USTIAN

Chairman, President, and CEO,
Navistar International Corporation

Establish "muscle memory." With enough iterations, a swing can be patterned without a conscious effort to remember it. Until that point, focusing on one, and only one, thought is necessary for success.

Lanny WADKINS

Twenty-one PGA Tour Titles
Champions Tour Player
Analyst, CBS Sports

The advice that got me playing very consistently came from Tom Case Sr., who was the pro at Sedgefield Country Club in Greensboro, North Carolina. I was in college at the time and his son, Tom Jr., and I played together at Wake Forest.

We were over at Sedgefield one time and his father gave me a little advice on my setup and my backswing. The key point was to maintain the flex in my right knee, which I had a habit of not doing. I worked on that for the next two or three years and prob-ably played the best golf of my life.

A good swing depends on the simple things

It's as simple as that. It's amazing—the top players will tell you it's the simple things, the alignment or some little wrinkle, that the rest of your swing revolves around. It makes all the hours that you work, and everything else, fall into place.

Tom WEISKOPF

Fifteen PGA Tour Titles
1973 British Open Champion
Two-Time Ryder Cup Team Member
1995 U.S. Senior Open Champion
Founder, Weiskopf Design

Some of the best advice I ever received came from the legendary Tommy Bolt. I was blessed with a very good golf swing and tempo; however, I had a very long backswing that went quite a bit past parallel early in my career. When under pressure, I tended to speed up my swing from the top, and I was a little bit loose at the top of my swing—somewhat out of control. Tommy told me to shorten my backswing, so as to not allow the club to get past parallel at the top of my backswing. This was what he called "quiet hands" at the top. I took his advice, which allowed me to slow down my swing, keeping the club on a critical path on the downswing and under control. This permitted me to control my trajectory and the distance of the shot required. After I learned this, I became a winner.

Slow down and shorten your backswing

The other tip from Tommy was "You can never control what anyone else does on the golf course. Eliminate anxiety and don't get ahead of the immediate shot that needs to be played. Slow down when the pressure is on."

Dr. Gary WIREN

*PGA Master Professional, Trump International
Golf Club, Palm Beach, Florida*

Deceleration is a swing killer! Think about it! You are on the eighteenth green with the pressure on and a six-foot straight-in putt for the win. Then "the choke stroke" attacks, your hands tighten, the club decelerates, and you pull the putt short and left of the hole. Or maybe it's a simple chip lying just off a fast running green. The thought of "too hard" grabs you in the backswing, your arms tighten, the club decelerates, and you hit far enough behind the ball to advance it only three feet. A similar result comes when you are in the bunker or the deep rough near the putting surface. Decelerate and the clubhead races forward as your arms slow, causing you to hit behind the shot. There is very little transfer of energy to the ball. The shot is a flub, a stub, a dunch, a chunk, a disaster. And then there is the tee shot. If you want to quick hook it into the bushes, just stop the forward swing of your left arm and deceleration will

Swing through the ball

take care of the rest. Then there is the drive. Tightening the hands and arms on a tee shot will guarantee you a loss of distance because undue grip pressure slows speed.

The answer? I received it from the late Toney Penna, PGA Tour player and club maker of note. After a round together, he once said, "Gary, golf is not a game of *to* . . . golf is a game of *through*." If the ball is causing you to add tension to your body that kills the swing, then you have to use your imagination. Imagine that you are going to get your greatest speed about a foot past the ball. It is a swing thought that two of the greatest players of all time, Ben Hogan and Harry Vardon, used because they realized that deceleration was a huge mistake. Don't just swing *to* the ball. Rather, swing *through* it, on both short and long shots. It will take you to a winning finish.

Golf
201

Dan BURTON

U.S. Congressman, Indiana

Over the years, I've received a lot of good advice about improving my golf game. I've been told to keep my head steady, to keep my nose behind the ball, to keep my back straight, to keep my left arm and wrist straight and firm through impact, and to follow through, among other things.

But I believe the best advice I've ever received is to

1. Have a game plan
2. Be relaxed
3. Have a slow backswing and follow through with consistent tempo
4. Not lose my temper

When I follow that recipe, my golf game almost always is better and more consistent—and I have a much better time at the nineteenth hole.

Glen CAMPBELL

Singer

The first time I took a lesson the guy told me to lay off for a couple of weeks and then quit. Even though it's great advice, I didn't take it. Besides a bunch of silly anecdotes, of which I've got plenty, the best tip I ever received was to pick a spot about two inches behind the ball on the ground. Try hitting it at that spot—you'll catch the ball a lot quicker and it's great for carrying a lot of slices. If you're out on the course and your game just isn't working, don't get stressed. Tell yourself a funny joke—that usually works for me—and get right back into the game with a relaxed state of mind.

Gary CARTER

National Baseball Hall of Fame
Celebrity Players Tour Member

My approach to golf before becoming a part of the Celebrity Players Tour was simply to go out there and see how far I could hit the ball. Then, finally, I took lessons with a PGA professional named Bill Scully, who has given me the best advice to date. It concerns three main things, which form the acronym "GAS":

> **G**rip
> **A**lignment
> **S**etup

I pounded many balls with him, and everything kept coming back to those three things. Once you focus on those, you take it back and have a good shoulder turn and try to swing at 80 percent power, rather than swing at 100 percent. That's the difference between the baseball swing and the golf swing. When you have the ball come at you at ninety-five miles per hour, your reaction is to be quick and swing hard, but for the most part your reaction time is less than a second. In golf, when the ball is sitting there on the tee, it is the concentration and GAS in mind with the 80 percent swing that gets you the best results.

> **A baseball swing and a golf swing are not the same**

Three things . . . one at a time.

Matt CLARK

Head Coach, Men's Golf, Georgia State University

Find your personality.

I always talk with my team about playing golf the same way you live life. If you like living on the edge, you probably do not enjoy laying up on a par 5 from 230 yards over water. You are probably more comfortable taking chances in life, so why not take them on the course? Once you find out who you are, take the same personality traits to the golf course.

Someone who rarely takes chances in life should have a conservative approach to golf. This person needs to map out the course and hit shots to conservative landing areas.

He also needs to be careful with the speed of his putting. If he has a twenty-foot putt and leaves himself a testy three-footer, his heart will probably start racing and the second putt will be extremely difficult for him.

This person also tends to be comfortable with tap-ins. On the other hand, someone who lives a fast-paced life will probably lose interest with this style of golf, so she needs to make sure she has a different approach. This person needs to take more aggressive lines on the course. Lag putting from twenty feet would only frustrate this personality type, so she needs to make sure she is more aggressive off the tees and on the greens. This style of golf will occasionally result in a big number, but it will also make more birdies and eagles.

Play to your personality

Are you someone who dissects the course and doesn't make mistakes, or are you an aggressive person who is going to pull out your three wood from 250 yards and make an eagle? Best of luck either way!

Derek HARDY

PGA Instructor, Long Beach Golf Learning Center, Long Beach, California

I am a golf professional and have been teaching golf for more than fifty years. I came to America in 1957 with my brother, who is also a golf professional.

Here are some of my favorite tips.

1. Asked why I charge $1,000 for a single lesson when I charge $300 for a whole series of lessons, I said, "If you expect a miracle, you should be prepared to pay for one."

2. One day I asked Shelley Hamlin, a well-known LPGA player who was my student, what she would say if she could leave something to posterity. She said, "There are two separate golf swings—a backswing and a downswing—and you must not join them together."

3. If I gave you Tiger Woods's golf clubs, it is fair to say that you would not play like him. The golf clubs do not make you a golfer. Tiger Woods's golf swing is developed by his brain and his body, and your swing is developed by your brain and your body. The only part of your body connecting you to the club is your hands, and they are holding the grip of the club. Learn to move your arms and body, and the club will do the correct thing. When the golf club left the factory,

> **Hands just hold the club**

it was highly trained. Most golfers have not learned to train their body.

4. All the hands do in a golf swing is hold the club. If you swing, the hands will take care of themselves.

5. All good golfers look like good golfers before they swing the club. The things you do before you swing the club are as important as the things you do during your swing: posture, grip, and aim.

6. "Ninety-eight percent of all putts that are short do not go in the hole."—English joke.

Arthur HILLS

*Past President, American Society of
Golf Course Architects
Managing and Founding Principal, Arthur Hills/
Steve Forrest and Associates*

The best golf advice I ever received relates to design. It's simple enough, but it works. And that advice is: design the golf course from the eighteenth green back to the first tee, not in the other direction. Find a place near a clubhouse site, find that green, go back to a good tee site, and keep on going. A corollary to this idea is to find the good green and tee sites and then figure out how to put them into a sequence. It is obviously pretty simple or it would be beyond my understanding.

In designing more than 185 golf courses, I would say that I adhered to this principle at least 90 percent of the time. Bay Harbor Golf Club in Petoskey, Michigan, and the Golf Club of Georgia near Atlanta are very good examples of finding the perfect clubhouse site, then weaving the golf course routing around that central location. The goal is then to find those natural tee and green sites that maximize the views while integrating the land's features and surroundings when framing the individual golf holes. I cannot think of a more challenging yet rewarding pastime. To see a great golf course come to life via this "reverse" orientation is one of life's treasures.

> **To understand the course, reverse your orientation**

Rick LaROSE

Head Coach, Men's Golf, University of Arizona

One piece of advice was from Jay Hebrew at Champions Golf Club in Houston, Texas. He was a great teacher, a great player, and a great champion.

While spending some time together at a junior tournament, we got to talking about the young players we were watching, and the subject of fundamentals in building a golf game came up. It was Jay's theory that a sound player would have a solid grasp of the basic fundamentals, including grip, setup, alignment, and takeaway.

I have always taken that message to heart when working with my players at the University of Arizona and the many young players I meet doing clinics around the world. I think any player can benefit from these basic fundamentals of the golf swing, which can help them to help themselves when their shots start going awry.

Confidence will lead to consistency

Keeping golf simple and basic certainly will allow the player to play better now and build a foundation for future improvement.

Another of my favorite advice stories comes from meeting Gary Player, one of the all-time greats of the game, while I was caddying for one of my players (Eric Meeks, 1988 U.S. Amateur Champion) at the 1990 Masters. During a practice round at Augusta, Gary said something that made some sense and which I found humorous, too: "Always blame your equipment. You can always get new equipment, but you will always have the same old you." Having confidence in yourself is critical in the game of golf. Gary Player certainly has confidence in his own ability. Keeping faith in your ability despite any adversity you might meet along the way is very important. I cannot think of too many people who have demonstrated confidence and consistency better than Gary Player has for so long.

Pierre LAROUCHE

Pittsburgh Penguins/Montreal Canadiens/
Hartford Whalers/New York Rangers, 1974–1988

When I was young, my dad always told me that the ball doesn't know where you're at, meaning you could be ten feet from the hole, or you could be two hundred feet from the hole. Don't worry where you're at—just hit the shot. Wherever it goes, it goes. He always said that when you play golf, you wish your opponents all the best and then you play your best—and at the end you see who wins.

I started playing when I was about six or seven years old. I remember my dad giving me a seven iron at the time and telling me to come back when I could hit it. That took two weeks.

Just hit the shot

Then I came back, and the old man gave me a two iron and said the same thing. I didn't see him for a year.

My dad was really good. I caddied for him and a couple of other people back home. They were tremendous skill players. There were no yardage markers on the course. It was all by feel.

I think that's part of the game that's missing now, playing from 150, 155 yards. I used to hit different shots all the time. That's what was nice about it.

Nancy LIEBERMAN

Basketball Hall of Fame
Analyst, ESPN

The best advice I ever received playing golf was to relax, try not to think too much, pick a spot on the back of the ball, then hit it.

"You're a great athlete," I was told. "You've got terrific timing, and if the ball does not go exactly where you want, you're still the best basketball player in the world."

And my response to him was "I'm not used to playing with short, white guys and I need a backboard."

Lynn MARRIOTT

Golf Magazine Top 100 Teacher
Golf Digest Top 50 Teacher

Every shot must have a purpose.

Greg "Piddler" MARTIN

PGA Tour Caddy

Golf, through the eyes of this caddy, is just like life, love, and business.

Ninety percent of the battle is just showing up. As us caddies say it: "Getting a job, finding a ride, and getting a place to stay."

We all live with imperfection. That is because we live in an imperfect world. Find a system that works for you—even if it's not perfect, stick with it. Remember: "An imperfect system worked consistently will always produce results."

Find a system and stay with it

For a baseball player to hit .300 means he makes an out seven times out of every ten times at bat. A good salesperson makes three sales for every ten calls he or she makes, and most pro golfers make 80 percent of their "big money" in 20 percent of the events they play.

As with life, love, business, and caddying, it is all about good work ethics. So, show up, know when to shut up, and always keep up!

R. Brad MARTIN

Chairman and CEO, Saks, Inc.

The best advice I ever received was from the entertainer Larry Gatlin. While we were playing together one day, he told me to "swing easier and learn to live with the extra distance."

Jennifer MILLS

Anchor, The Golf Channel

Here's a big one: If you're holding up the group behind you, let them through! We all know the frustration of playing the "let me through" game.

Telltale signs that your group is slowing progress:

There is a lot of daylight in front of you.

The group behind you is within one shot (you're in the fairway, they're on the tee; you're on the green, they're in the fairway).

The individuals giving chase have "assumed the position" (one hand on the hip, the other leaning on a club, legs crossed, and they're coughing loudly and often).

Finally, you start getting pelted with incoming golf balls.

Legendary college basketball coach John Wooden told his players to "be quick without hurrying." The same principle applies in golf.

Tim MORAGHAN

Director of Championship Agronomy,
Rules Department, USGA

One afternoon while trying to master hitting a draw on the practice tee at the golf club that our family grew up on, my father—a fine player in his time—simplified my game by stating to his headstrong son, "What's wrong with straight?"

When I began my career with the USGA, I split time between the Green Section—our turf advisory department—and the Rules Department. Mr. Bill Bengyfield, who at the time was the national director of the Green Section, summed up turf management to me, a former golf course superintendent, in a nutshell, by exclaiming, "Nothing occurs faster in agronomics than crop failure."

Stay within your limits

And after I explained to my friend Mark O'Meara how I'd failed in my attempt to get close to the par 5 fourteenth green at Pebble Beach in two shots, and bemoaned hitting a three-wood out of bounds, making a 7 and ruining my chance at a career round, he calmly questioned my tactics by asking, "What was your second-shot yardage?"

I told him it was three hundred yards.

"What is three hundred yards?" he asked. I told him I didn't understand his point.

"Three hundred is a hundred and sixty-five plus a hundred and thirty-five," he said. "Next time, hit six iron and then nine iron. And stick to your day job."

Kevin NEALON

Former Cast Member, Saturday Night Live

"Always go back to your bag to get the right club for the shot, no matter how inconvenient."

It makes sense, though. What if a surgeon didn't go back to his tray for the right instrument while performing surgery on you? You wouldn't want him or her to use a scalpel when he or she should have gone back for a laparoscope. By the same token, you wouldn't want to take an aspirin for a panic attack when you should get up, put your slippers on, and go back to your medicine cabinet for a Xanax. I think you get the idea.

I'm sure that guy had more advice for me, but he went back to his bag to get another club and never returned.

Pia NILSSON

Golf Magazine *Top 100 Teacher*
(coach of top players, including Annika Sorenstam)
Golf Digest *Top 50 Teacher*
Captain, 1998 European Solheim Cup Team

It's not about you or your swing—it's about the target!

Andy NORTH

Two-Time U.S. Open Champion
Champions Tour Player

My first piece of advice: When I got started playing, the most important point made to me was to go out and have a ball playing, to enjoy the fact that I was spending time with interesting people in a wonderful environment. That's pretty much how I approach playing golf. My first recommendation for others is to have a great time and enjoy the surroundings.

My second piece of advice: I was lucky enough early on that my father and Lee, the pro I worked with, made an effort to make sure I understood the importance of having a rhythm to my golf swing. Remember, if you are trying to hit the ball so hard that you are falling down, you're probably not going to have the rhythm you need to hit it well.

Tom PATRI

Owner, Tom Patri Golf Schools
Golf Magazine *Top 100 Teacher*

I had the good fortune (really good) to be invited by an old college teammate, Tad Weeks, who is the head professional at Champions Golf Club in Houston, Texas, to come visit. Tad also arranged for me to spend some time with Jackie Burke Jr. Jackie, for those of you who call yourself golfers and don't know who he is, well, try tennis, and while you're at it say hi to Bill Tilden! Mr. Burke won some little gathering in April outside Atlanta called the Masters, and the PGA as well. Enough said. I couldn't wait to pick Mr. Burke's mind, of course, wanting to hear the "secret" of the golf motion— I just knew he would share it with me. When the correct moment arrived, I pounced.

Golf revolves around three clubs

"Mister Burke, what did you work on in your swing when you played the tour?"

With zero hesitation, he turned to me and said, "Driver, wedges, putters!"

I thought that he didn't understand my question, so I restated it: "No, Mister Burke, I mean, what did you work on in your game?"

He looked at me slightly cross-eyed. "I said, driver,

wedges, putter." He went on to say, "Look, Tom, if you can't drive the golf ball, can you compete?"

"No, Mister Burke, definitely not!"

"Tom, if you can't wedge the ball at a higher level, can you compete?"

"No way, Mister Burke, no way."

"Tom, if you can't putt at a very high level can you be very competitive?"

"Mister Burke, I get it!"

He went on to say that he basically practiced those three clubs and felt that golf and the playing of the game revolved around them.

Today, as I develop my junior students and college players, guess what I focus on with my kids? I feel we teach far too much golf swing and coach "how to play golf" far too little. The art of hitting shots and controlling ball flight is an unknown commodity to today's youth. Wedge play and putting are also lost art forms in terms of creativity/feel. Mr. Burke and the great players and teachers of that generation had wonderful eyes (no video to depend on!). Today's players and teachers have become lazy with the use of technology. My best advice to you is to make golf a more creative endeavor.

Stone PHILLIPS

Anchor, Dateline NBC

I love golf. And I firmly believe that I am on the verge of taking my game to a whole new level. I have felt this way for approximately fifteen years. Here are the best golf tips I ever received.

"You might think about loosening your grip."
—Paul Azinger, after seeing my blood-soaked golf glove

"Get back on your heels and hit the f——— out of the ball."
—John Daly

"When putting, address the ball with one hand on the club and both eyes on the cup. Open the face of the putter and slowly rotate it counter-clockwise until settling on the exact line."
—Steve Elkington, Ph.D.

Take advice from as many sources as possible

"Just because your feet are square to the target doesn't mean your shoulders are. Get those shoulders square!"
—Johnny Bench (brilliant!)

"Try it again. And this time, just give me 80 percent."
—Doug Mauch, golf instructor extraordinaire

*"Come to a complete stop at the top of the backswing.
And drink more Oregon pinot noir."*
—**Mary Jo McCloskey**, women's varsity
golf coach, Lewis & Clark College

"Consider playing tennis."
—**Don Grief**, friend and golf buddy

"Forget everything I just told you and enjoy the game."
—**Jay Haas**, my first PGA Tour pro-am
partner and a wise man, indeed

Denis POTVIN

Hockey Hall of Fame

I walked into a pro shop and was looking for new clubs because, like most everybody else who plays at my level, I feel that when you're not hitting or striking the ball well, the clubs are wrong. Even the putter's not so good.

So, I walked in and spent $1,500 to buy a new set of clubs. Before the golf pro had me sign the credit card, he looked at me and said, "Denis, you know, these are great golf clubs. But how many good golf lessons could you get for fifteen hundred dollars?"

Basically, the bottom line is it's not the club's fault.

Brian SILVA

Partner, Cornish, Silva & Mungeam, Inc.
Golf Digest*'s Architect of the Year, 1999*
(designs include Chattanooga's Black Creek Club,
ranked in Golfweek*'s 100 Best Modern Courses)*

For two decades, I've done public speaking on golf course architecture—at Harvard, at USGA functions, industry conferences, you name it. One of my presentations, "The Five Frontiersmen," follows the careers of the five individuals who have wielded the greatest influence on the history of golf course design. For twenty years, I have told audiences a Pete Dye anecdote: When he designed Harbour Town on Hilton Head in South Carolina, he desperately wanted it to be different so that he might develop his own, unique reputation. He surely accomplished this. In my opinion, his innovations and his traditional use of angles "saved" the craft of course design in the late 1960s.

Little did I know that Pete had planted that thought—the desire to do something distinct—in my own mind. It led to a significant departure in my own design work in the late 1990s. This new direction led backward to the "traditional" American designs of the early twentieth century: much wider playing corridors, random bunkering positioned perpendicular to play, an emphasis on the ground game around the greens (as opposed to modern dartboard design), and, every once in a while, a classic golf hole feature like a redan or punch-bowl green. Like Pete's departure, mine relied on the blending of design characteristics from decades past to create something distinct.

During the summer of 1997, I worked on two Massachusetts projects—Waverly Oaks in Plymouth and Cape Cod National—that offered me perfect jumping-off points. Two years later, when Ron Whitten of *Golf Digest* named me Architect of the Year, he explained the choice: Of all the architects who told him they were designing "traditional" courses,

> **Don't be afraid to do something new**

Cape Cod National and Waverly Oaks were the first two he had seen that actually delivered on this theme.

Awards are nice, but even more important, I was now fashioning courses that caught my own fancy and reminded me of the vintage courses that to this day remain my favorites and my inspiration. Thanks, Pete.

Debbie STEINBACH

CEO, Venus Golf, Inc.
Golf for Women *Magazine Top 50 Teacher*
*Author, Motivational Speaker, and National Golf
Spokesperson for Rally for a Cure*

Like most people, I'm always happy to give advice, but not always happy to receive it. But there are exceptions, and this particular humbling piece of advice came early in my career as an LPGA Tour player and it has stayed with me through the years.

When I first started competing on the tour in the late 1970s, I was fortunate enough to sign on with a leading firm called International Management Group out of Cleveland, Ohio. The creator and mastermind of IMG was an intelligent and powerful lawyer, the late Mark McCormick. Mark was well known even then for being the agent for the most famous golf pro of all, Arnold Palmer. In 1977, as a new IMG client, I was invited to join Mark and Arnold for dinner during the Colgate/Dinah Shore Winner's Circle Golf Championship.

As we were finishing our meal, Arnold asked me what I had shot in the final round of my last tournament. I didn't want to tell the world's most famous and popular golfer that I had closed with an embarrassing score of 80, so I proceeded to ramble on and on about what a tough course it was, how the greens were unfair, my tee time was too early, my pairing was lousy, blah, blah, blah. Finally, Arnold held up his hand and

Don't make excuses

told me he had heard enough. He had some "advice" for this new-and-upcoming tour player. He spelled out loud and clear that when someone asked what you shot, you should just answer the question and spare the details! Nobody else is interested in your "story." Arnold went on to point out that if I wanted to see a bunch of "losers," all I had to do was go into any locker room at the end of a tournament round. I would see all the losers gathered there, talking about their rounds, making excuses and replaying each and every shot for all their fellow losers to hear. Then Arnold said that if I wanted to see some actual "winners," all I had to do was head to the practice range after the tournament round. He said the winners would be back out on the range working on their golf swings for the next day. Winners accepted and took responsibility for their scores, whatever they were, then moved on. (Sounds a lot like life.)

When he had finished, Arnold asked me again what I had shot. I looked the King squarely in the eyes and answered with one word: "Eighty." He smiled and replied, "Too bad. I am sure you will do better next time."

Not only did Arnold Palmer's advice have a profound effect on me, but hearing it from the King himself with Mark McCormick at his side made it a lasting lesson I will treasure forever. It is no surprise that Arnold and I have stayed friends to this day.

Golf is a metaphor for life, so the next time someone asks you what you shot after a poor round of golf, accept responsibility for your performance by simply looking that person in the eyes and giving your score—that's it, nothing more!

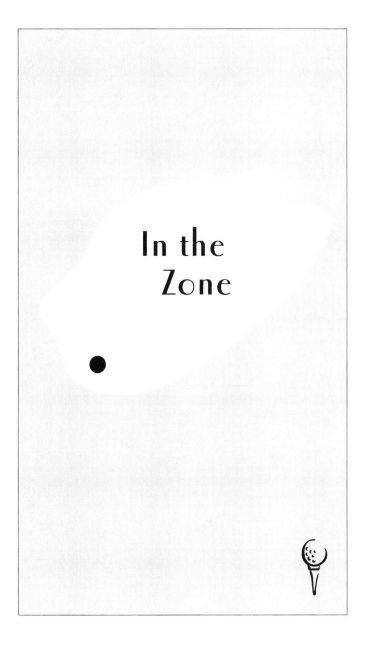

In the
Zone

Yogi BERRA

National Baseball Hall of Fame
Major League Baseball's All-Century Team

One time I was complaining that my shot was going to wind up in the water. So my friend Kevin Carroll told me that I should think positive. I told him okay, I was positive my shot was going to wind up in the water.

Jane BLALOCK

Twenty-seven LPGA Tour Titles
Record Holder of Most Consecutive Cuts Made
on Both the PGA and LPGA Tours
Commissioner, Women's Senior Golf Tour

As I reflect on my eighteen-year career on the LPGA Tour, I can very honestly profess that my positive attitude was more responsible for winning tournaments than my actual golf swing. Two distinct comments, which must be credited to the two people who played a critical role in my success, make up the best advice I ever received.

The first was from Tom Nieporte, currently director of golf at Winged Foot in Mamaroneck, New York: "Play each and every golf shot as if it were the final shot to win the tournament." To elaborate, there is a tendency for golfers even on our level to play with a different level of intensity during various stages of a tournament, so to focus one's energy singularly in preparation for every shot will eliminate lapses that result in poor shotmaking.

The second piece of advice was from Bob Toski: "Always use poor and inclement weather conditions to your advantage, as the majority of players in the field will succumb to the excuses and negativity that permeate the locker room and clubhouse on difficult days." As a result of this advice, I welcomed the poor conditions and always felt that I was given an advantage.

Use bad weather to your advantage

The greater the grumbling and complaining, the more I smiled, knowing I would bear down just a little bit harder. This is truly the art of turning a negative into a positive. The golf course always rewards those who can "weather any storm!"

Kenneth H. BLANCHARD

Author, The One Minute Golfer:
Enjoying the Great Game More

The best golfing advice I ever got was from Spencer Johnson, my coauthor on *The One Minute Manager.* He taught me all about time orientation when he was working on his brilliant parable, *The Present.* His focus was on life, but isn't that what golf is all about? I think G.O.L.F. spells Game Of Life First. The big message in *The Present* is that we need to learn from the past but not live there. We need to plan for the future but not live there, and we are the happiest when we are in the present.

Elaine CROSBY

Two LPGA Tour Titles
Former President, LPGA

Immediately after I graduated from the University of Michigan, I worked at Saginaw Country Club for two summers. I had only been playing golf for four years at the time—I had always been a tennis player.

Saginaw Country Club held an outing to benefit the Girl Scouts. Kathy Whitworth and Sue Ertl, two accomplished LPGA players, came to give an exhibition and invited me to be part of the group. Later, at the luncheon, I was sitting next to Kathy, and she inquired about my future plans.

"I'm not really sure," I answered, "but my dream would be to play on the LPGA Tour." But I then went on to say that I started playing golf so late that I didn't think I could catch up to everyone else.

There is more than one way to turn a dream into a reality

Kathy told me to do everything I could to make my dream a reality. "There is always more than one way to get on the LPGA. Everyone goes about it in a different way," she said. "If you really want it, you can make it."

I've always remembered that advice and given it myself to others who are trying to fulfill a dream—no matter what it is. There is more than one way to skin a cat. (Though that's really a disgusting saying!) One year later, I made the LPGA Tour and enjoyed sixteen years competing on the circuit.

Manuel de la TORRE

PGA Instructor,
Milwaukee Country Club

Stay in the present.

The present is the golf swing. Good swings produce good shots. Good scores are the result.

Tom DOAK

*Architect (designs include Pacific Dunes Golf Course
in Oregon and Cape Kidnappers Golf Course in
New Zealand)*
Author, The Anatomy of a Golf Course,
The Confidential Guide to Golf Courses,
The Making of Pacific Dunes
Coauthor, The Life and Work of Dr. Alister MacKenzie

The best advice I ever received about the golf business came from Brian Morgan, the golf photographer, when I was embarking on a year overseas to study the great golf courses of the British Isles. Brian told me that because golf was a relatively small industry, limited-edition works were the most prized and the most profitable, whether photographs (his area of expertise) or golf courses. I've found that to be true in everything I've done—from publishing a book on golf course architecture *(The Confidential Guide to Golf Courses)* myself to

> **Stop complaining and keep it positive**

striving to make my courses individual works of art instead of so-called brand-name designs that could be mass-produced.

The best advice I ever received about playing golf was something said to me by Walter Woods, the superintendent of the Old Course at St. Andrews, Scotland. He was giving me a tour on my first day in the country, and I asked him if golfers complained about the natural mixture of grasses found in the putting greens on the Old Course. He said very simply, "The good player will see that, and allow for it." It was a typically pragmatic Scottish reply, but in a larger sense it is the very essence of positive thinking, which is a habit of good golfers everywhere.

Bob GOALBY

Eleven PGA Tour Titles
1968 Masters Champion

The best advice I ever got probably came from the first guy I went to work for when I turned pro—Jackson Bradley at Edgewater Golf Club in Chicago, a wonderful course. I knew Jackson pretty well, but I didn't have much confidence about my game.

Jackson told me, "Bob, you got to believe in yourself. You're better than you think you are. You can really play." I had never played in a pro tournament until I went to work for Jackson.

I happened to qualify for the U.S. Open that year, 1953, and I finished in the top twenty-four; that got me an exemption for the rest of the year—for the rest of my career, really.

Dr. Deborah GRAHAM

Cofounder, GolfPsych
Coauthor, The 8 Traits of Champion Golfers

Early in my practice as a counseling and sport psychologist, I was unable to find relevant data for enhancing the performance of golfers, leaving me determined to research their personalities. To generate the data, I administered a standard personality assessment measuring thirty-two specific traits to dozens of willing participants on the PGA and Champions Tours. In the process, I found eight distinct personality traits of champions, as well as a treasury of wisdom about golf and life. My findings were not advice, per se, but served the same function as advice in helping me to develop ways to work with professional athletes.

Maintain a peaceful and quiet mind

Through a number of players who knew him, I learned of Ben Hogan's determination to make the most of a given moment. Hogan had learned from experience that looking ahead or behind in the round hurt his performance. To avoid these pitfalls, he employed imagery. One of the most vivid images was of a tall and strong brick wall behind him, which prohibited his looking back in the round. Hogan poignantly demonstrated this in his life as well, refusing to look back with regret and defeat. In so doing, he exhibited the champion's traits of focus and tough-mindedness.

Fred Couples illustrated for me the importance of maintaining a peaceful, quiet mind for decision making and shot execution. When he felt his mind getting busy with mechanics, outcome thoughts, or worries about what other people thought, he instinctively knew he needed to get "quiet" and relaxed before his next shot. He found the answer in what psychologists call object meditation. He would find one of the biggest and most interesting trees, then calmly outline it with his eyes, thereby distracting, quieting, and relaxing himself in preparation for his next shot. Fred's ability to manage stress/arousal so well has, at times, left him open to charges of indifference. That's unfair. His skills have enabled him to conquer the stress of injury and personal loss to forge an enduring career. Fred's actions display the champion's traits of quiet mind and optimum arousal.

Josh GREGORY

Director of Golf/Head Coach, Men's Golf,
Augusta State University

The best advice that I have ever received as a player is one that I share with my college players on a regular basis. Whether you are a 25 handicap or a PGA Tour player, you should be able to use this strategy. It never seems to fail that before a tournament round or even a noncompetitive round with your buddies at your local club, you always hit your best on the range and everything seems to be clicking just right. Your swing feels great; you are hitting that perfect five-yard fade or draw, whichever your desired ball flight is. Of course this is the case—there are no nerves, no pressure, no hazards, no out-of-bounds stakes . . . only positive thoughts. You have such high hopes heading to the first tee. Then, all of a sudden, things change; you now realize that all of your shots count. Everyone, no matter what level, has experienced first-tee jitters. The difference between a world-class tour player and top amateur is the ability to "take it to the course."

Golf would be a lot more fun if we always had our A game when we stepped on the first tee; however, that is not always the case! Invariably, it takes a few holes to figure out what game you are going to have that day—your A, B, C, D, or F game. The best players in the world are able to figure out quickly what game they have that day. In other words, **Play the game you bring that day** "play with what you have that day." For example, your normal ball flight might be a slight draw, but on the first three holes you have hit nothing but push fades. Instead of hoping to hit the slight draw that you were hitting on the driving range, why not play with what you have that day—the push fade. There is always time to work on swing mechanics after the round. During a round of golf, your thoughts should be simple—"see the target and react to it." I stress to my players all the time about determining what type of game they brought to the course each day. The day when you bring your A game is the day you fire at every flag, take drivers off holes you might otherwise hit irons, and see how low you can shoot, because those days are few and far between. For a PGA Tour player, this is turning a 68 into a

64 or lower. Those days when you bring your C game or worse is when you just try to hit the center of the green, take few unnecessary chances, and try to get the best score possible out of your round. For a PGA Tour player, this is turning a 75 into a 70. These are the days when he or she wins the golf tournament. That is what the top players in the world do—they always get the most out of their round. They figure out what game they brought to the course that day, and they go with it!

The thought process of "play with what you have that day" should help the high handicapper or the tour player. It takes just a few swings or a few holes to figure out what game you brought to the course that day. The quicker you figure it out and go with it, the lower your scores will be.

Ron GRESCHNER

New York Rangers, 1974–1990

At first, they told me golf was really easy. But then I never figured out how a little ball like that could beat me up so bad and humiliate me, being so much smaller than I am.

The funny thing is I like the game. I've been playing for ten or eleven years. I enjoy the game and I'm above the grass. I had a couple of back operations, so that affects my swing. I just play. I'd like to be able to swing like other people do, but with my back, I'm just happy to be able to hit the ball. I enjoy the game. Win or lose, I play as hard as I can, but I don't get upset if somebody beats me.

Mike HOLDER

Head Coach, Men's Golf,
Oklahoma State University

After many years of playing, instructing, and coaching golf, I have come to the conclusion that "less is more." Complicated thoughts or advice usually produce negative results.

Tony JACKLIN

1970 U.S. Open Champion
1969 British Open Champion
Two Champions Tour Titles
World Golf Hall of Fame

Growing up in the 1950s in England, I didn't have the benefits of television or video to learn about golf. I was self-taught. In my early teens, I came across a poem that was to be an inspiration to me. In fact, the original copy is in the World Golf Hall of Fame in St. Augustine, Florida.

If you think you are beaten, you are.
If you think you dare not, you don't.
If you'd like to win but you think you can't,
It's almost certain you won't.
If you think you'll lose, you've lost.
For out in the world you'll find success begins in a
*   fellow's will, it's all a state of mind.*
Life's battles don't always go to the strongest or
*   fastest man, but sooner or later the man who*
*   wins is the man who thinks he can.*

Peter JACOBSEN

Seven PGA Tour Titles
2004 U.S. Senior Open Champion

The best golf advice I ever received was when I was an amateur player and embarking on my PGA Tour career. It came from Bruce Cudd, a friend of mine from my hometown of Portland, Oregon. Bruce had played a few years in the PGA Tour, and he told me that his attitude had kept him from having a career because he would get so upset with how he'd played and always look back and play the "what if I'd made that putt" and "if I'd hit that shot better, I would've made the cut and made X amount of money" head game with himself.

The advice he gave me has served me well over the past twenty-eight years on tour. He told me to go out there, play the first two rounds of any tournament, and if they tell you you've got a tee time on Saturday, go play. In other words, don't count the shots that you played poorly and don't count the shots that you played well—just play the first two rounds and if you make the cut, you play on the weekend. You play Saturday and Sunday, and when they give you a check on Sunday, take it, put it in your bank account, and don't look back. The worst thing you can do is to look back and have regrets over the shot you played, the decision you made, or the putts that you missed or misread, because that kills the spirit and kills any opportunity you have to be positive and to count on yourself and to have confidence in the future.

Play without regrets

So I have taken that advice. More than golf swing advice, more than course management advice, more than advice given by legends of the game, I look to Bruce Cudd's advice as the best I've ever received. Simply move forward, don't look back, don't play the "what if . . . could've . . . should've" game. Just keep moving forward.

Dan JANSEN

1994 Olympic Gold Medalist, Speed Skating

The best golf advice I ever received came from my wife, Karen, who happens to be an LPGA teaching professional. My years as a speed skater in a very technical sport have transferred to golf in that I'm always worried about my technique.

When I think about this too much, I never play well. Her advice to me was very simple but very wise:

"Work all you want on the technical aspects of your game while you're on the range, but when you are on the golf course, stop getting in your own way! Play the golf course and trust that the work on the range will carry over to the course. It will take time, but nothing comes quickly in golf."

John KRUK

Analyst, ESPN's Baseball Tonight

I used to have a bad temper, throwing and breaking clubs, and my brother said to me, "Why do you get so upset? If you were any good, you wouldn't be playing with us, you'd be playing on TV."

Siri LINDLEY

2001 ITU World Triathlon Champion
World Ranked Number One Female Triathlete,
2001– 2003
Analyst, NBC Sports

The best advice I ever received in golf was to not over-think. I got so caught up in trying to remember every little detail that would lead me to the perfect stroke that I became too tense and thought way too much, and it was destroying my game. By paying attention to doing things properly but relaxing more and just going more by feel, I played so much better and had a lot more success.

Derek McDONALD

PGA Instructor, Echo Lake Country Club,
Westfield, New Jersey

You must see the target in your mind's eye while you are striking the ball. It takes a lot of practice, because you always want to focus on making contact with the ball. But you make a smoother swing through the hitting area when your mind is focused on the target rather than the ball. You tend to achieve a more fluid swing because you don't get distracted by the mechanics of the swing.

Jim McLEAN

Owner, Jim McLean Golf Schools (the number one golf school in the United States)

The best advice I ever received came from golf legend Jackie Burke.

While I was attending the University of Houston and playing on a team with future PGA Tour stars like Bruce Lietzke, Bill Rogers, John Mahaffey, Fuzzy Zoeller, and Keith Fergus, I often drove up to play Champions Golf Club built by Burke and Jimmy Demaret (a three-time Masters Champion himself).

One day I stopped in Jackie's office to ask him about driving. Without saying much, Jackie suggested I drive down to Galveston and hit a few balls into the Gulf of Mexico. That was the end of the conversation, and I left not knowing what the heck he meant.

About a week later, a few of my teammates and I drove to Galveston for a rare "beach day." This was a fifty-mile drive from Houston. While we were there, I remembered Burke's advice. So I went back to my car and pulled out my driver and three golf balls. The beach at Galveston, if you haven't been there, is very firm, so teeing a ball up was no problem. I hit the three drives not knowing what I was trying to do. That was it. I brought my driver back to the car and didn't give it another thought until I visited Champions again several weeks later.

By then, I had almost forgotten about those three tee shots into the ocean. But when I passed by Jackie's office and saw him in there I remembered.

So I walked in and said, "Jackie, I hit those balls with a driver into the Gulf."

Mr. Burke quickly replied, "What did you learn?"

I must admit I was not ready to answer, so I just said, "I'm not sure." He then asked how I hit the shots. I replied, "I hit all three balls great."

Visualize the ocean and just let go

Jackie jumped out of his chair and said, "That's it, you dumb SOB. The secret is to completely let go, pretend you're hitting it into the Gulf of Mexico every time, and for you, McLean, think of the Atlantic Ocean, because as you know it's about fifty times bigger than the Gulf."

I never forgot that advice, and it has saved me several times in key pressure situations. It's something I even teach my pro students. You can't be a good driver if you steer the ball. You have to let it go.

Joe MORGAN

National Baseball Hall of Fame

Dave Stockton, the great former golfer, and my cousin, Walter Morgan, who played on the Senior Tour for a long time, gave me the best golf advice I ever received.

Basically, they told me I am who I am. I can't be Ernie Els. I can't have that long, slow, smooth swing because of my build and my height. My rhythm is always gonna be my rhythm. Find that rhythm, and whatever rhythm allows you to get the clubhead through the hitting zone is what you should do. You don't try to smooth it through or be slow if your personality is one of aggressiveness. They just said your swing is gonna fit your personality, and I found that to be true over the years.

When I watch Ernie Els, what's his personality? Kind of soft and smooth. Tiger swings hard. His is more of a violent swing because he's aggressive.

Accept what kind of player you are

That's what they said to me. Your personality will set the tempo of your swing. I found that to be true, and I've played pretty well throughout my career.

Both of them said that you can't imitate someone else. Whatever your personality is, that is what you have to be. That philosophy was better than the swing tapes I've gotten through the years. Their advice stuck with me.

Linda S. MULHERIN

PGA Master Teacher
Golf for Women *Magazine Top 50 Teacher*

When under pressure, we need to distract the conscious mind from mechanics, fear of failure, and first-tee jitters. Pick a phrase that has nothing to do with golf, then say it over and over again as you begin your preshot routine. If negative thoughts start to creep in, you may have to say the phrase aloud to distract the conscious mind. By preoccupying your brain with the phrase, you keep out negative thoughts. This helps your physical body to go on what I refer to as "automatic pilot," freeing your body to react to the target and swing freely, not inhibited by negative thoughts.

Over the years, I have put myself on automatic pilot to deal with an important three-footer, the first tee in a local PGA event, or even after a lesson when I have a lot of mechanics in my mind. The best thing about this advice is it works. So, the next time you're on the range, pick out your phrase and work on using it while hitting golf balls so that you're committed to the process before you use it on the golf course.

Phil NIEKRO

National Baseball Hall of Fame

I'm not a real good golfer. Probably the same philosophy I used when I played baseball I used in golf.

I learned in baseball to accept your losses without being defeated, and I think I learned in golf to accept my bad shots without being defeated. I don't play real competitive golf. I play in a lot of golf tournaments and in some bragging-rights tournaments. I'm not good enough to play competitively against anybody.

Don't let yourself be defeated

I've got that handicap where I get enough shots in the course of a match to play someone who's fairly good. If I have a good game, I can beat him. If he has a bad one, we're pretty competitive.

In my whole life, I never played golf when I played baseball. I didn't want to mess anything up. I didn't start playing golf until I got out of the game. I could be better, I know I could. It's just like on the field. The more you work on the field, the better off you're gonna be; and the more you're out on the golf course, the better golfer you're gonna be. It's a good, relaxing game for me.

Jim PALMER

National Baseball Hall of Fame

I have a good friend by the name of Mike Adams. He has written all kinds of books and is one of the most respected golf pros in the country.

One day, I was taking a lesson from him and he looked at me and said, "You read a lot of golf books, don't you?"

I said, "Oh, yeah, I have a whole library full."

He said, "You have a lot of golf videos, don't you?"

I said, "Yeah."

He said, "You probably watch the Golf Channel, don't you?"

I answered, "Oh, yeah, every chance I get."

He said, "I'm gonna tell you one thing, give you one good bit of advice. Go home, get all those books, and put them in a box. Go home, get all those videos, and put them in another box. Go home, call your cable company, and discontinue the Golf Channel. Bring both boxes down to me and I'll start the fire."

> **Throw away your golf books**

Then he looked at me and said, "If you had as many pitching thoughts as you had golf and swing thoughts, you would have won forty-eight games instead of two hundred sixty-eight."

Gary PANKS

*Architect (designs include Turtle Point Golf Course
in Australia, Twin Warriors Golf Club in New Mexico,
and Grayhawk Golf Club and Sedona Golf Resort
in Arizona)*

As an architect, I am self-taught and did not have a mentor, but I learned a lot from observing the work of others. I worked on a number of courses with the Australian golf champion David Graham, who was the only Australian to win more than one major in the United States. He won the 1979 PGA Championship and the 1981 U.S. Open.

When we were designing courses together, David advised me to place my hazards on the insides of doglegs and to raise the outsides to help turn the holes. He recommended not making my designs too penal under perfect conditions, because when the wind kicks up such penal courses become unplayable for most golfers. He also warned against placing too many hazards in front of greens, because most golfers aren't skilled enough to carry them.

Banish all negative thoughts

I also believe that too many bunkers on the golf course can ruin it for everyone. You need enough to properly define the fairway landing areas and green targets, but not so many as to confuse the golfer and clutter the landscape. This doesn't include waste bunkers, which act as ground cover in rough or out-of-play areas. I usually design for forty-five to fifty bunkers on a championship-length golf course. At the end of the day, the architect often gets favorable comments from low-handicap players, but if we don't hear the same from players of lesser abilities we have not done our job.

In addition to being a golf course architect, I'm also a player with a passion for the game. The best advice I have received as a player came from Dick Riley, a former amateur champion in Arizona. He taught me to visualize and verbalize the shot at hand and never allow a negative thought, even as the subconscious mind sometimes tries to take you there. This supports my own observations that you should play the shot you have the most confidence in and not ask too much of yourself. The best way to deal with pressure is through good concentration.

Gary PLAYER

Three-Time British Open Champion
Three-Time Masters Champion
1965 U.S. Open Champion
Nineteen Champions Tour Titles
Recognized as the "International Ambassador of Golf"
World Golf Hall of Fame

Throughout my fifty-year golfing career, I have traveled extensively and have often received very valuable advice. All of this advice can be summed up by what I call my "Three-Dimensional Approach."

The Mental Dimension

Over the years, I've learned that this game challenges one's mind anew every single day and presents one with the ultimate opponent: yourself. I am often asked, "Why play golf?" and I reply, simply, "Why *not* play golf?" Anyone can do it, and the rewards to the mind, body, and soul are endless.

A friend of mine once told me: "Simply by making the effort to start something, you will be miles ahead of almost everyone else. After that, the key to success lies in your determination."

The more I play golf, the more I'm inclined to think that the mental factors have the greatest bearing on actual success. *The Power of Positive Thinking,* by Norman Vincent Peale, gave me great mental inspiration at a time when I needed it most.

> **The harder you work, the luckier you get**

The Physical Dimension

My father often advised me of the benefits of physical strength and flexibility. Even though I was a very keen athlete from an early age, I only realized the need for a daily exercise routine after I played the Masters in 1957. Golf requires a sound base of physical preparedness. There is no doubt that the physical dimension is the most difficult aspect for golfers to sustain.

The Skills Dimension

Ben Hogan was a great inspiration in motivating me to practice and develop a balanced swing technique. He always said, "The secret's in the dirt." My interpretation of this is "the harder you practice, the luckier you get." This embodies the idea that nothing worth achieving comes easily. Just look at Vijay Singh.

On reflection, my golf career, and whatever success has come with it, has taken many years of hard work, dedication, and determination. And I've loved every one of them!

Karl RAVECH

Host, ESPN's Baseball Tonight

The best advice was from Chi Chi Rodriguez: "Avoid paralysis by analysis. Turn your brain off. Stop thinking so much out there and just see it and hit it."

Cindy REID

Golf for Women *Magazine Top 50 Teacher*
Director of Instruction, Tournament Players Club at
Sawgrass, Ponte Vedra Beach, Florida

When you spend ten hours a day giving golf tips to other people, you're pretty discriminating about the tips you receive. I've been given thousands of golf tips in my career, but the one that stands out the most came from a friend and neighbor of mine in Ponte Vedra, Florida, who also happens to be the number one ranked golfer in the world.

When he's not on the road, Vijay Singh practices at the Tournament Players Club at Sawgrass, the course where I'm the director of instruction, so we spend a good deal of time together on the range. He rarely offers swing advice, and, as tempting as it is, I never ask. He works on his game and, when I'm not teaching, I work on mine.

The one exception to that unwritten rule came late one winter afternoon when we had both spent much of the day toiling on the mechanics of the golf swing—Vijay working on his own game, and me trying to coach and encourage others to play better. As I gathered up my teaching aids and put my own clubs back in the bag, I said, "What are you working on, Veej?"

"Routine," he said without looking up.

I watched for a few more minutes before saying, "What about your routine?"

Rarely am I this brazen when talking with tour players, but Vijay and I have known each other a long time, and I've always found him to be not only kind and generous, but also forthcoming with his wisdom and insight on the game. He stopped his practice and propped himself up on his club as if it were a cane, crossing one foot over the other to strike a relaxing pose.

"The golf swing is about repetition," he said. "In order for the swing to repeat, you also need to repeat every move leading up to the swing."

This was the standard definition of a preshot routine, one I had been teaching for years. You always start from behind the ball; you pick your line; you move into your address position; you check your aim; you look at your target; you go through a preset number of waggles, and you swing. Every shot with every club requires the same preshot routine. It wasn't until I listened a little closer that I realized Vijay was discussing more than simply the mechanics of a good routine.

"Not only do you have to have a consistent physical routine, you also have to have the same mental routine before every shot," he said. "When I'm standing behind the ball before I address it, I always visualize the shot I'm going to play—not just the line, but the trajectory, and how the wind should affect the shot, where it should land, and how the ball should react once it hits the ground. I try to feel the shot before I ever take my stance. That way I'm totally committed to the shot before I address the ball."

Repeat every move leading up to the swing

I'd heard and read about visualization before, but I'd never heard anyone put it in the context of your preshot routine the way Vijay was describing.

"I can be as physically prepared as anyone in the world, but unless I'm confident in my mental routine, the swing I've worked on out here won't repeat when I get to the golf course. The physical routine is only part of it; you've got to have a mental routine that you can repeat just as consistently as your golf swing."

From that moment forward, I incorporated Vijay's mental routine into my practice and preshot ritual. I start every swing from behind the ball, just as I always have, but instead of picking a line and letting my mind wander, I go through a regimented visualization drill before each and every shot.

The results have been astounding. I'm hitting more fairways and more greens than ever before.

I don't know if Vijay would characterize this tip as his "secret" to great golf (he's not shy about sharing it with anyone who has the patience to listen), but I know it is the best golf tip I ever received, and one I'll be teaching to my students for years to come.

Dean REINMUTH

Former PGA Tour Player
Golf Magazine Top 50 Teacher
Founder, Dean Reinmuth Golf Schools

The difference between good players and great players is much more than just hitting a golf ball. In my forty years of playing and teaching the game to PGA Tour champions, top corporate executives, celebrities, and avid golfers, I regularly impart to my clients what I believe is the best golf advice I ever received—"play each shot as a separate game."

The ability to view each shot as its own unique challenge, or a game within the game, is the key to being able to assess the risk-reward relationship to determine the proper shot for your ability. Arnold Palmer wrote a book several years back, *Go for Broke*—but although it was a clever title, it doesn't reflect the way the game is played. I once gave a note to one of my young tour players that read, "Never let your emotions dictate your decisions."

It's important not to be afraid to hit the shot you need to hit, but it's critical to only hit the shot you have the ability to hit. As a general rule, those who go for broke usually end up that way. Only by playing each shot as a game within the game can you learn to manage your risk, allowing you to minimize your mistakes and enable you to come back from the adversity the game dictates.

Stay calm, cool, and collected

Maxann SHWARTZ, Ph.D.

Licensed Psychologist/Venus Golf, Inc.
Golf for Women *Magazine Top 50 Teacher*

As a former competitive golfer, I, like many golfers, have sought out advice on how to get into "the zone," which is that elusive, magical place that we as golfers have all experienced when we play our very best. Now, as a clinical psychologist and golf instructor, I advise students of all abilities, including tour professionals, on how to improve their mental game and play in the zone.

Every human is capable of reaching this focused mental state by playing in the moment. This requires getting out of your head and into your senses. This is only achieved by letting go of unnecessary thoughts, both past and future.

Playing in the moment does not take effort; rather, it takes an act of letting go of effort.

Recently, I worked with an LPGA Tour professional who was desperately trying to recapture her past success. The harder she tried, the worse she got. She was so attached to her results that despite a golf swing that had won numerous tour victories, she was unable to perform under pressure. Her personal challenge was not to add more information or change her swing but rather to let go of her fears and expectations. By submitting to the process of letting go, she dramatically improved her game, her confidence soared, and she was able to win again.

Play in the moment

Although the process of letting go differs for each of us, the answer always lies within. When we are playing golf, unnecessary thoughts and feelings often act as distracters. When we are able to stay focused in the moment, we become free to enter into the zone. From here, the possibilities are endless, as you become free to play your best.

So let go and let's golf!

Vijay SINGH

Twenty-four PGA Tour Titles
2000 Masters Champion
2004 PGA Tour's Player of the Year

You know, I've been given a lot of advice, but probably the best is the simplest: do it yourself. A man in Jacksonville, Mike Flemming, told me that. He worked with me a little bit, and he's an old-timer, and he said you just have to go out there and find yourself—keep it simple. You don't need to get your golf swing by going through video cameras and stuff like that. Just kind of go out there and find yourself. The old saying goes "finding it in the dirt." I think that works the best for me.

J. C. SNEAD

Eight PGA Tour Titles
Four Champions Tour Titles

The year was 1968, and I had only recently joined the PGA Tour. The advice sounds so simple but put in the proper context it can change your game. My uncle, the legendary Sam Snead, told me, "Play within yourself."

He was giving me advice on my iron play and those three simple words would change the way I approached my iron shots. Playing within yourself means finding a smooth, balanced rhythm that is as natural to you as possible. In other words, don't hit at the ball too hard. If you take this advice, you will find more control over your distance and direction, and if you do miss hit, it won't go too far off line and you are less likely to hit flyers. For example, my typical nine-iron shot before was 165 yards. With my new approach, it was 125 to 135 yards, but it made all the difference in my game. There have been many occasions when my irons have made the difference in what would have otherwise been a less than stellar performance.

John STARK

CEO, Stark Carpet Corporation

Just hit it.

Kelly TILGHMAN

Anchor/Reporter, The Golf Channel

As a longtime host of our prime-time instructional show, *Academy Live,* I've had the privilege of standing next to many of the finest golf instructors the world has ever known. Greats like David Leadbetter, Jim Flick, Bob Toski, Rick Smith, Dean Reinmuth, Jim McLean, and Dave Pelz grace our stage regularly. These people are truly geniuses when it comes to dissecting and communicating the complete anatomy of the golf swing. I've welcomed to the show world-renowned mental experts like Bob Rotella,

Trust your game and the pieces will fall into place

Rick Jensen, Fran Pirrazzollo, Gio Valiante, and Deepak Chopra. As a journalist, I've been fortunate to be able to interview some of the game's best players while they were at their peak—Tiger Woods during his 2000–2001 stretch, Annika Sorenstam after shooting 59, and Vijay Singh following his nine-win season in 2004. Not one of these players possessed the same swing thought while notching those grand achievements.

Surely the best golf advice I've ever received came from *one* of these legends, right? The answer is no, it came from *all* of them. Even though every one of these accomplished professionals approaches the game in a completely different manner, they all share one common belief. You're at your best on the golf course when you're just trusting it. Have you ever noticed that when you take a lot of time off from golf, the first few holes of your next round are usually your best because you don't possess any swing thoughts? It's not until you realize that you're 1 under par through five holes that it all begins to fall apart.

"Trusting it" is the goal of every swing coach, every sports psychologist, and every touring professional. With enough practice, you can patent any motion and let nature take its course. When Annika shot her 59, she told me she was just trusting her motion and concentrating on shooting 54. During Tiger's 2004 stretch when he was undergoing big changes in his swing, he continually stated that he was close. It was just a matter of trusting it. When Vijay Singh ended Tiger's five-year reign as the number one player in the world at the 2004 Deutsche Bank Championship, he said he hadn't been thinking about his golf swing all year because all of his hard work was allowing him to trust it. David Leadbetter can enlighten you with little-known facts about the golf swing. Dr. Bob Rotella can provide you with the mental tools to compete alongside the world's best golfers. You could even discover the famous secret to Ben Hogan's well-studied swing. All of this priceless information could send you to a new level . . . but only if you trust it.

Mardell WILKINS

Former LPGA Tour Player
LPGA Club and Teaching Professional

When I was a young player on the LPGA Tour, I frequently had a blowup hole or two that ruined my score for the day. I was paired a couple of times with JoAnne "Big Momma" Carner when this happened.

I had a number of opportunities to play practice rounds with JoAnne, and she was always willing to offer advice to a younger player. At one point during the round, she pointed her finger at me and said, "Do you know what your problem is?"

As you can imagine, this really got my attention. "No," I meekly replied.

"You are not willing to take a bogey," she said. "You are so worried when you hit a bad shot that you take an unnecessary risk to try and make up for it, and then you turn a bogey into a double or worse. Everybody makes bad shots and bogeys," she told me, "but you have to believe that you can make a birdie to recover from it."

Learn to live with a bogey

I took her advice to heart and learned to make a safe recovery when I was in trouble, to be willing to live with a bogey, and the result was a lowering of my scoring average.

I never forgot this advice, and today as a teacher I frequently share this advice and this story. Perhaps this is one of the reasons I have been chosen as LPGA Western Section Teacher of the Year twice!

Bob WOOD

President, Nike Golf

Golf is a game that everyone struggles with at times . . . especially me. If you're like me, then you're a person who's a perfectionist, incapable of reaching anything close to perfection on the golf course. So, like many type As, I have struggled to hold my temper at times on the course when things were not, shall we say, exactly going my way.

You are the only one who cares about your score

The fact that I was allowing golf to be that frustrating at times posed a problem for me since, as the president of a golf company, I am expected to play with others from time to time and am responsible for representing my company in an appropriate fashion. Not to mention the fact that I'd like to enjoy myself once in a while. So, I really struggled with that until my good friend and golf teacher Christopher Smith let me in on a little secret.

Nobody but you cares how you play.

Really, everyone else couldn't care less. And, as long as you don't act like you care, no one's the wiser. I think half the reason people get angry when they play poorly is that they are embarrassed. But if you remember that nobody cares, you realize that there's a lot less to be mad about and you'll relax.

Get
Tough

Jim L. AWTREY

CEO, PGA of America

When I first wanted to play the tour, some veteran players told me to get tough. They said half the players out here don't care what you shoot and the other half wish you had shot higher! It was at this time that I learned my wife, Jeanne, was my most loyal friend and supporter.

Wayne DeFRANCESCO

Golf Magazine *Top 100 Teacher*
Golf Digest *Top 50 Teacher*

In 1972, I was a fifteen-year-old hotshot junior golfer who was used to either winning tournaments or at least playing well enough to be in the hunt at the end. I was playing in the Tournament of Champions that year, an eighteen-hole stroke play event, and I was paired with a seventeen-year-old whom I knew to be a good player, although a bit on the wild side when it came to on- and off-the-course behavior. I thought he was cool, and in the back of my mind I wanted to impress him with my play. Unfortunately, both of us played poorly on the front nine, and when we both hit our balls out of bounds on ten he looked at me and said, "I'm out of here. You want to go get a beer?" I thought about it for a moment and, knowing that I had no chance to win and excited about possibly impressing my friend by joining him, I decided to blow off the tournament and head for Pizza Hut.

I didn't think much about what I had done until the junior golf awards dinner at the end of the season, about three weeks later. The guest speaker was Marty West, a Walker Cup player and local amateur legend. I was sure he was looking directly at me when he said that "the one quality all the great players have, and the one that all of you will need in the future, is that of perseverance. To persevere is to never give up, to never quit, no matter how far out of the running you may be. If there are holes left to play then you can birdie them all, and by giving it your best no matter what the circumstances and continuing to grind it out you can often turn things around."

Don't take the easy way out

Marty told me many years later that he was not talking specifically to me, but I sure took his message to heart. My career as a player has had innumerable ups and downs, with multiple back surgeries precluding my attempt to play in the PGA Tour. My love for the game has persisted, however, and whatever success I have had (including winning the National Club Professional Championship in 2001) has been a direct result of my ability to overcome injury, disappointment, and failure by remembering Marty's words: never give up.

Fred GRIFFIN

Golf Magazine *Top 50 Teacher*
Director, Grand Cypress Academy of Golf

Never give up on a hole. Even though you might hit two, three, or four bad shots in a row, you might hole out your next pitch, chip, bunker shot, or putt to save your score.

Natalie GULBIS

LPGA Tour Player

Believe in yourself—this applies outside of golf as well. In addition to teaching me the many technical elements of the game, my father also instilled in me a strong work ethic and a mental toughness. He would remind me each day to believe in what I was doing, to trust in what my coaches were telling me and to apply their lessons with the belief that they would help me reach my goals. He was right. I qualified for the LPGA Tour at age nineteen on my first attempt, believing that I belonged out here. Confidence is a powerful tool, and I hope that you apply it to your game.

Rich LERNER

Host/Reporter, The Golf Channel's
Golf Central

More than forty years ago, my father, Les, and several of his friends opened a golf center in Allentown, Pennsylvania—an eighteen-hole, fully lighted par-3 course, a miniature golf course, and a driving range. It was called Dorneyville Golf Center.

My three brothers and I worked there from about age twelve through our early twenties. We operated the cash registers, planted flowers, picked up trash, played pinball, and whacked golf balls. We hired mostly our friends to round out the staff.

The pro was a local legend, a gruff hustler whose golf lessons were brutally simple and to the point. In his sixties with silver hair slicked back over a balding pate and an impeccable tan, Frank Stocke gave me the greatest piece of advice I've ever heard.

A teenage golfer of some promise, I'd often return to Frank to get straightened out after some high-priced teacher had tied me in knots. "Frank," I'd say desperately, "my spine angle's off, my swing plane's just not where it needs to be, and when I set my wrists early it feels funny, plus at impact my club's getting trapped behind my body. What do you think?"

Stop thinking and just hit the ball

"Hit the fuckin' ball," he'd bark in a deep smoker's baritone, a blue-gray stream of smoke racing from his nostrils, the unfiltered Camel dangling from the corner of his mouth. And I'd swing away, released from my confusion.

Even today, when I'm overloaded with information and muddling around like a head case, Frank's voice cuts beautifully through the clutter.

John MAGINNES

PGA Tour Player
Three Nationwide Tour Titles

When I turned pro in 1991, I sought the advice of several people. My circle of friends was rather small and the only two people I knew that had ever played a PGA Tour event were club pros from North Carolina. Both had played back in the day of the rabbit, when there was very little money and even less prestige.

One of these men was the head pro at the most affluent club in Durham, North Carolina. The club is Hope Valley and the pro is a man named Johnny Cake. We have never been close; however, he has always been incredibly supportive whenever I come around. I sought his advice for two reasons. One was his experience; the other was because the richest people in my hometown were members of his club and I needed sponsorship. I never did get the sponsorship, but what I got was a nugget of wisdom that is not only true in golf but, I have come to learn, in life and business as well.

I spoke with him on the putting green behind the plantation-like clubhouse at Hope Valley. Johnny is a small man like most pros of his era. He is maybe five feet eight inches and slim with a wisp of dark hair and the manners of a southern gentleman. I had never heard him swear in my life prior to this conversation in 1991 and never again since. The question I posed was simple.

"Mister Cake, I am going to turn pro in a couple of weeks. What do you think?"

"Why?" was Johnny's only reply.

"Because I have to. I don't have any choice. It is all I ever wanted," I said feebly.

"Okay, damn," he muttered under his breath and turned away. After a long pause under the shade of the century-old oaks, he finally turned back to me. "If it's in your blood, then you need to know something I learned from Tommy Bolt. Playing as a professional is a lot different than playing as an am. Even the best ams have friends. When you play in a professional event and you make a nine—and believe me, if you play long enough you will make a nine somewhere along the way, they all do—but when you are playing as a professional, ninety percent of the field doesn't give a shit that you made a nine."

You have few friends when you are playing for money

With that he turned back off the putting green and took several steps toward the Pro Shop. I was bending over to hit another putt when he turned one final time and said stoically, "The other ten percent wish that you had made a ten." After a few beats he added, "Good luck, kid."

Janice MOODIE

LPGA Tour Player

When I was fourteen years old, my mum told me she was going to sell my clubs if I didn't play more often. That was pretty good motivation for me.

Kyle PHILLIPS

Architect (award-winning courses include Kingsbarns Golf Links in Scotland and The Grove in England)

I have found two pieces of advice, offered to me by two mentors, to be very helpful in my career as a golf course architect.

Working with Robert Trent Jones Jr. for more than sixteen years provided me with enough memories to write a book. But when I sat down with him in June 1997 to inform him that I was resigning to begin my own practice, he gave me some simple advice that I will never forget: "There will be many times that a decision will not be obvious and many people will be giving you their advice. Kyle, you have good instincts, so remember in the difficult situations to trust your instincts."

The other piece of advice came from Mike Lin, now one of the best-known graphics teachers in the country, who was a professor of mine in college. Every student, regardless of how talented at the beginning of Mike's rigorous course, was greatly improved by his graphic techniques and sometimes harsh, but always honest, critiques. One of his goals was to get students to loosen up and not fear failure. Mike was always buzzing around the studio and had something to say about everyone's work. One day, on a routine pass by my station, he saw that I was discouraged and ready to quit and start over on a project. He took one look at my work and then stood back and shouted, "Good, you have almost ruined it! Keep going, keep going, because you are almost finished!" Sure enough, I kept working, and the final result was one of my best.

Trust your instincts

Patty SHEEHAN

Thirty-five LPGA Tour Titles
Two-Time U.S. Women's Open Champion
Six-Time Solheim Cup Team Member
LPGA Hall of Fame
World Golf Hall of Fame

I grew up in a wonderful family. My parents gave me great basics to live by. My mom, Leslie, was quite an athlete in her own right, having been a downhill and cross-country skier. My father, Bobo, was also a fine athlete in his youth, having played basketball, baseball, and football, and participated in ski racing. He was a great coach at Middlebury College in Vermont for twenty-two years in sports such as baseball, football, golf, tennis, and skiing, and was also the U.S. Olympic ski coach in Cortina, Italy, in 1956.

Stay strong and go get it!

When I was just eleven years old, I ski raced for a team in Lake Tahoe, California. One time in a downhill race when my dad was standing there watching, I caught a ski tip coming out of the starting gate and spun around 360 degrees. Before I had a chance to stop spinning and possibly quit, he bellowed, "Boot it!" Not wanting to disappoint him, I took off as fast as I could. The only race I didn't win that year was that one, in which I finished fourth. I have used "Boot it!" as the mantra for my life. "Boot it!" has always meant "Go get it!" The lessons we learn from our failures are often even more valuable than the experience we gain from our successes.

To this day, my family continues to inspire and motivate me. Through their constant support, I am able to accept change and frequently look for new opportunities. "Boot it!" embraces the belief that success does not come merely by wishful thinking. I have two beautiful children of my own. I can only hope that I can impart these same values and morals to them and that "Boot it!" will be an inspiration for everything they choose to attempt in their lives.

Ben WRIGHT

Emmy Award–winning CBS Golf Announcer,
Author, and Golf Course Designer

The best golf advice I ever received was from my paternal grandfather, Arthur Wright, secretary of the Triumph Motor and Motorcycle Company, who gave me a cut-down, hickory-shafted mashie he had made with his own hands—a beautiful thing. I was a World War II hellion at the time—my tenth birthday—and my grandfather, on a card presented with the gift, said:

"In the forlorn hope that by playing golf you might finally achieve even the thinnest veneer of civilisation, I commend you to use this club in my back garden."

Alas, the Coventry blitz intervened in November 1942, so I had a short session in the aforementioned garden. But I quickly developed a passion for the game that has never left me, although today it has become a love-hate relationship as I slide into my dotage.

Game
Time

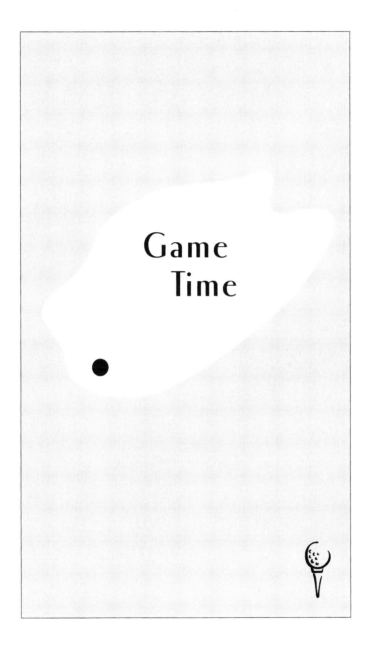

Paul AZINGER

Twelve PGA Tour Titles
Four-Time Ryder Cup Team Member

The best advice I ever got was from Byron Nelson at Inverness in 1993. Nelson had been the pro there and told me that the greens were so small I should ignore the flags and shoot for the center of the green. That way, I would have plenty of birdie opportunities. I believe I led the field that week in greens in regulation and, of course, won the PGA championship.

Brandel CHAMBLEE

PGA Tour Player
Analyst, The Golf Channel
Spokesman for Quiet Feet Golf Training Equipment

The best golf advice I ever received came from my father shortly after I had begun playing. I wanted to qualify for the high school team, which was pretty ambitious given my skill level, and I was understandably nervous. My father was driving me to the course about a week before the qualifying and said to me, "Son, whether you make the team or not has no bearing on your future in this game. It's a small hurdle, and whether you clear it or knock it down doesn't matter. What matters is your commitment to the game and your attitude. If you don't make the team, we'll find tournaments for you to play in."

In a couple of sentences he alleviated my anxiety and put a few rounds of golf in perspective for me. Years later, I was talking to Bob Rotella, the premier sports psychologist in golf, and he said to me, "To play your best golf you can't be concerned with the outcome, you have to fall in love with the process. Embrace it." Truer words were never spoken, and I realized the advice I was paying Dr. Rotella for, my dad had given to me for free. The devil is in the details, so to speak. Get a plan, put your head down, go to work, and love every minute of it.

Put the game in perspective and enjoy the journey

By the way, I qualified for the team.

Orrin HATCH

U.S. Senator, Utah

The following advice has been very helpful to me as I have tried to at least adequately play the game of golf.

1. Take the time to get your mind set for the golf game on each particular course.

2. If you can, play every hole in advance in your mind.
3. Imagine every shot and that you could hit every shot properly and well.
4. Believe that you can do it.
5. Warm up by hitting every club—especially the putter.
6. Test the greens for speed and resistance before starting your round.
7. Don't worry about the score—just play the game and give it your best.
8. Wear back support and swing easily.
9. It doesn't pay to get mad and swear, no matter how rotten your opponents may be to you.

Per-Ulrik JOHANSSON

Two-Time Ryder Cup Team Member (Europe)
Five European Tour Titles

The best advice I've ever gotten (and given) involves the need for good course management.

Get the Most out of Every Round

Contrary to what you may think, playing on tour isn't always about hitting huge drives, making towering iron shots, and sinking every putt you look at. Even though all of us are pretty good technicians these days, every top player has developed the skill of squeezing every single last drop of potential out of his or her round—most of the time!

At the very top level of the game, the ability to keep your score ticking over while avoiding the disaster holes is the secret to playing good golf and finishing near the top of the leaderboard. The good news is that many of the tricks of the trade that I have developed over the years are just as relevant to you—the amateur club golfer. Here's a selection of ideas, swing thoughts, and playing strategies that you can absorb into your own game right now to become a much better player.

Straighten out Doglegs from the Tee Box

Very few golfers use the full width and depth of the teeing area. In fact, most amateurs simply tee up in the middle of the markers and aim somewhere down the fairway. On a dogleg hole to the right, setting up next to the left-hand tee box gives me the angle to cut through the corner of the dogleg, which is something that I couldn't do if I had set up on the right-hand edge.

Always think about where you want to play your approach shot from in the fairway and then work out which area of the teeing ground gives you the best angle and the most margin for error.

Be Pin-High with Approach Shots

I like to know the exact distance to the hole at all times. This is because it is vital to be pin-high with your approach shots. It's unrealistic to expect to fire every single approach shot directly at the flag; more often than not, you will either pull or push the ball slightly. While a ten-yard pull to the left of the flag may look disastrous in the air, if you get the distance right you will often be pleasantly surprised when you walk onto the green and find that you have left yourself a relatively straightforward twenty-to-thirty-foot putt. However, if you are ten yards left and ten yards short of the pin, chances are you'll leave yourself a tricky chip shot or even a pitch for your next shot.

Adjust Club Selection According to the Condition of the Greens

One of the most important keys to scoring well is taking many possible factors into account on each and every shot. Take your approach shots, for example. The condition of the greens plays a very important role in influencing your club selection. If the greens are wet, you can fly your seven iron 140 yards or so through the air and it will stop stone dead on landing. If, on the other hand, the greens are as hard as concrete, you may need to use an eight iron or even a nine iron to get the ball to travel the same distance, since it will bounce forward and run ten to twenty yards on landing.

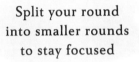

Split your round into smaller rounds to stay focused

Think about the state of the greens, plus the wind and even the temperature, when you evaluate your shots. Remember that the ball flies considerably farther in warm air than in the cold.

Know the Yardages

Many golf courses these days have the yardages etched onto sprinkler heads at various points in the fairway, yet what does the figure mean? Is the yardage to the front of the green, the middle, or the back? Chances are you probably don't know. Check in the pro shop before you go out to play to find out what the yardages refer to. The distance from the front to the back of the green can be forty or fifty yards at times—the difference between hitting a seven iron and a three iron.

Put the Past Behind You

There are a lot of things that you can't afford to do if you want to remain on tour for any length of time, but dwelling on your bad holes is one of the quickest ways to miss cuts. I know how easy it is to get frustrated and upset after making a double bogey—especially at the start of your round—but you have to put the hole behind you and start thinking about the next one straight away.

A technique that I use to stay in the present is to split each round into six groups of three holes. I then set myself a target of playing each set of three holes in 1 under par. That way, I always have something positive to focus on, and bad shots are quickly forgotten. You can set your own targets according to your ability.

Terry LUNDGREN

CEO, Federated Department Stores

1. Ask your caddy if he knows how to read the greens well. Tell him it is okay if he doesn't, but you would prefer to know before, rather than after, an important putt. If nothing else, he will work hard to give you a good read.

2. Play fast. Pick up when you are out of the hole unless you are putting for par.

Patricia MEUNIER-LEBOUC

LPGA Tour Player

The best golf advice I ever received was in fact a piece of tennis advice from my father: "Your goal must be to make your ball pass over the net once more than your opponent." I was ten years old and my pleasure came mostly from the result, whatever the means.

When I started to play golf, I again focused on the outcome. I thought I needed a perfect swing and worked pretty hard to achieve it. As I had a winner's state of mind, I was successful most of the time, but my body and my brain had to fight hard to send the ball to the right place. To raise my game to the highest efficiency, I quickly felt I needed a less stereotypical game, a more creative game, closer to my true personality.

When I turned professional, I decided to work with Corinne Soulès, who was still playing on the European Tour at that time. She presented to me the best association between hard work in practice and its application in tournament playing, giving a large role to feelings. She first began to help me stiffen and broaden my game, giving me all the technical weapons I lacked. Then she taught me to use them on the course in a different way, to play golf fluently, a game more sensible, spontaneous, and balanced, allowing me to be able to choose the best among several solutions when the score counts. And the tennis advice found its mirror in golf: "On the course, whatever you have worked on, you must play with what you have in store. The more you have worked, the more you will master your shots and the more you will have in hand different solutions. Among them, you'll have to choose the best one you feel you can deal with at that moment to make the shot happen."

On the other hand, when I must play a shot without the feeling of having all my weapons and past experiences on hand, my swing turns tense and jerky; I spoil my energy and golf begins to be unpleasant work. The pleasure in playing a shot is missing, and my ball "doesn't pass over the net anymore!"

Be prepared to adapt yourself to all conditions

Today, more than yesterday and hopefully less than tomorrow, when going from practicing golf on the range to playing golf on the course, my ultimate goal is to create shots that give me an intense pleasure. When they are added on the scorecard, they lead to better scores. The outcome remains the main pleasure, but each shot is experienced as a new manner in which to express myself, as another pleasure in itself. I seek some excitement in anticipation of the shot, a kind of inner vibration. Even if I don't have my best swing at the time, I know how to adapt myself to all the conditions. I can succeed because of all the long, hard work I have undergone.

Pleasure without result is not enough for me, nor is result without pleasure.

Walter MORGAN

Three Champions Tour Titles

As I ventured on the PGA Senior Tour (now the Champions Tour) in 1991 after receiving my exempt status card, I received a phone call from Charlie Sifford (recently inducted into the Golf Hall of Fame) welcoming me to the tour. He advised me as I traveled to always find comfortable, quiet hotel accommodations, get proper rest, and eat wholesome meals. Above all, he instilled in me the importance of good golf course management.

My wife, Geraldine, has been my total support system, encouraging me to keep God in my life, believe in myself, and keep a winning spirit. I always take time to practice the weak areas of my game, think positive, and when playing a round of golf, put my focus on one hole at a time. I never dwell on my mistakes—I just pray, meditate, and keep the faith. "What is faith without works; what is work without faith."

Bob MURPHY

Five PGA Tour Titles
Eleven Champions Tour Titles

Advice is ever present and readily forthcoming. On the tour, there is a constant interchange of thoughts. You actually find advice going into your head from surrounding conversations. Dangerous!

So, my best advice came from my teacher, Conrad Rehling. He said, simply, that advice and/or suggestions from just anyone could be confusing. "Stick with what we do and do it well."

We did!

Kevin SPRECHER

Lead Master Instructor, Jim McLean Golf Schools

"Don't believe everything you read."

In other words, in golf, "Do not believe every piece of advice you hear." Just because you read some tip in a golf magazine or book, or watch a golf video or hear a commentator give an opinion on television, that doesn't automatically mean the advice is good. Therefore, do the research yourself. Study videotape and still photos of the great players to see what is really happening. Believe your eyes and use your common sense to understand what you see and hear.

Remember, when looking at videotape, everybody sees what they want to see. Players will often describe what they are feeling or trying to achieve in their golf swings. However, it might not actually be happening as they describe. It is not always possible to match an image to human action. So remember these words of advice: "What they feel is not always what they do" and "What you hear is not always what you see."

Douglas TEITELBAUM

President, Bay Harbour Management

Winning tournament play from the worst golfer with the greatest tournament record:

My advice is written specifically for guys like me who have not devoted the time to really learn the game but who enjoy it and play in tournaments at least once every three years.

The golfer who plays less than infrequently has a big advantage in tournament play. I have managed to win many trophies and prizes over the years.

My advice is as follows:

Do not attempt to store your clubs—get excited about your golf outing by fully outfitting yourself anew each time you play. No one else on the course has a consistently fresh set of clubs each time they play; besides, you will never find your once-used old clubs when you look for them anyway. I'm talking clubs, shoes, glove, great putter, and many, many, many balls.

Do *not* go to the driving range and practice in the weeks or days leading up to your tournament outing. Golf, like gambling, rewards the newcomer as a way of bringing you back for the beating that is to come in the future. You can defeat this by taking advantage of first-time luck. Go fresh to the course for your outing and just hit thirty minutes of practice at the driving range that day.

Rely on beginner's luck

Only play in low-net tournaments.

Only play two-man golf with scratch or near-scratch golfers. I will not play in a tournament with anyone who has a handicap above 5. In a low-net game, the infrequent golfer only needs to contribute three holes when playing with a really good golfer. This has consistently worked for me. Standard logic says that you want strokes in a low-net game. This is not the case with two-man low-net golf tournaments. Really great golfers will play the course consistently and will give you fantastic course and club management advice, and you will do your part by just playing a few holes really well. I usually can birdie one hole and par two holes on a given round. With my handicap, and with consistent play by my partner(s), this can be ideal. When you play in four-man tournaments, the strategy changes a little. You must have one scratch player and two mid-handicap players. Those mid-handicap players have a lot of shots and will play, on average, six fantastic holes. If you get lucky, and everyone's great play doesn't match up, this combination can be lethal. I have used it many times. I won the Bear Stearns High Yield Golf Tournament four times in a row using this simple structure.

Michele TRIMARCHE

LPGA Master Professional
Golf for Women *Magazine Top 50 Teacher*

1. Practice does not make perfect. Perfect practice makes perfect. So any drill you do, any motion you make, do it correctly. Otherwise, you are wasting your time and energy.

2. Don't be misled into thinking that the best players hit all good drives and all good second shots. Golf is a game of misses. The best ball strikers on the tour hit about thirteen greens in regulation each round, which means they miss five. Learn to manage your misses and you will see your improvements in your score.

Perfect practice makes a perfect game

3. Be prepared to scramble, right from the first tee. This is great advice, because it readies you to face adversity and use your mental toughness to look at every difficult on course situation as a challenge.

4. Golf is 50 percent mental, 40 percent setup, and 10 percent swing.

5. Naturally, the best of instructors cannot construct or even overhaul an entire swing in one lesson.

6. A child can play golf well; an adult will never master it.

7. Play the shot you can play best, not the shot that would look the best if you could pull it off.

8. Commit to the target and lose all responsibility.

9. Eighty percent effort and 100 percent commitment.

10. I've got it, I had it, I lost it! That just about sums up the frustration the fickle game can muster in all of us.

Lori VAN SICKLE

PGA Master Professional

I always encourage my students to focus on the shot that they are making and how that shot will set up the next shot. As instructors, we concentrate on one shot at a time, which is important; however, we must get the student and ourselves to see how that shot will impact the next one (i.e., hitting a ball to the left side of the fairway so that your approach shot will take away a water hazard or other obstacle). Manage your game one shot at a time, keeping in mind the impact of that shot on the next.

Maury WILLS

MLB Two-Time Gold Glove Winner
National League MVP, 1962

I've always been an avid golfer, and the game is still my passion today.

Once, when I was about to tee off, a couple of people I didn't know approached me. One of them asked if I wanted to wager on a game against him. I walked over to my friend, who was a golf pro at the course, hoping he could give me an idea of what my odds would be in this situation. He wisely told me to find out whether the challenger had a job.

"If he has a job, you can beat him," he said. "If he doesn't, you probably can't."

So, out of all the years I've played golf, I'd have to say the best advice I ever received is not to make a wager with someone who doesn't have a job.

Mergers and
Mulligans

Joe BEDITZ

CEO, National Golf Foundation

Over the years, I have seen hundreds of avid golfers who were very successful in their chosen field (business, law, medicine, etc.) try in vain to turn their avocation into their vocation. I've seen retired doctors squander their life savings trying to build golf courses. I've seen otherwise successful businessmen waste loads of time and money trying to bring unnecessary golf inventions to market. I've seen a retired state supreme court justice bang his head against the proverbial wall trying to bring a golf business idea to fruition. And I've seen many, many investors sink good money after bad into failed golf ventures (bankrupt golf equipment companies, golf magazines, golf course developments, etc.), only to suffer failure themselves.

In all these cases, these bright, successful people had their good business judgment go missing because of their passion for the game. So the best advice I've ever *given* is to keep golf your avocation and forget about making it big in the golf business.

Gene BERNSTEIN

Principal/Owner, Northville Industries
Cofounder, Champions Tour Commerce Bank
Long Island Classic

Although I have played golf for some forty-four years, the best lesson I have learned from the game occurred about eighteen years ago when my father, brother, and I established a Champions Tour PGA tournament on Long Island, the Northville Long Island Classic (now in its eighteenth year and called the Commerce Bank Long Island Classic). Moreover, the lesson came not on the golf course, or even the practice range or the putting green. The lesson came as the tournament drew to a close the first year (1987) and the volunteers began to migrate toward the last hole. After the final putt was made, the check and the trophy were handed out, and champion Gary Player made his remarks, dozens of volunteers approached me to say, "Thank you."

A game can bring out the best in people

I was stunned. These were the people whom the tournament organizers and sponsors had to thank, not the other way around, or there would have been no event. But these good folks—many of whom were golfers themselves, and others who had never played the game but simply wanted to help out the beneficiary (the local chapter of the American Cancer Society) raise money, or help the local community prove that it was worthy of a world-class sporting event—these people were thanking me for starting the tournament. Some of them had used vacation time to get up at five in the morning so they could be at the airport to pick up an arriving pro, or put in twelve to fourteen hours of volunteer work at the driving range. I felt so indebted to them, but they showed how a golf tournament could be a great civic event that brought out the best in people from all walks of life—executives marshaling a hole with bus drivers, doctors manning a medical tent with cafeteria workers, you name it—all pulling together because of what a golf tournament could and did mean to their community.

Jeffrey BRAUER

Architect (designs include Giants Ridge Golf Resort, Minnesota, Golf Digest*'s 2004 Best New Upscale Public Course, and Avocet Course at Wild Wing Plantation, South Carolina,* Golf Digest*'s best new course winner)*
Former President, American Society of Golf Course Architects

When I decided to start my business and was trying to explain my business plan to my father, Arthur Brauer, a Campbell's soup sales manager, he said, "If you can't explain it in three sentences or less it probably isn't a very good business plan, and talking about it more doesn't make it any better. You ought to be able to articulate it clearly and simply. Otherwise, it's not likely to work."

He was my toughest critic, and as I was trying to sell the concept to him, he kept asking, "Why is this going to work and why is this service needed?"

I went to the local public library and looked for cities in the South where I thought golf would boom, and Dallas was the only one without a golf course archi-

Keep it short and to the point

tect listed in the phone book. So I said, "I'll be the only one in town."

He said, "Okay, I understand that concept. You're beating the competition by avoiding it."

Robert CATELL

CEO, KeySpan Corporation

The best golf advice I ever received was given to me by a friend, who told me:

"Golf is very much like business, full of hidden surprises and unexpected outcomes. In order to be successful, you need to have a game plan, stay focused, concentrate, don't get discouraged, and play to win."

Caleb CHAN

President and Chairman, Burrard International, Inc.
President, GolfBC

The best advice I ever received is that the game of golf is a microcosm of the game of life. The values that guide one's life should guide the way one plays golf: with integrity, honesty, respect, and enthusiasm. I strive to run my golf courses with this in mind so that the golfers who play my courses go away having had a fun yet valuable experience. My hope is that I can create an atmosphere in which people learn to love the game of golf like I do.

Geoffrey CORNISH

Partner, Cornish, Silva and Mungeam, Inc.
(designed more than two hundred original layouts;
renovated hundreds more since 1952)
Fellow and Past President,
American Society of Golf Course Architects

The best golf advice I ever received came from two people, on separate occasions, before World War II. It concerned my profession, namely golf course architecture, a calling that seems to hold magic and mystery for many. That identical advice was "If you really want to comprehend your life's work, teach it—in the classroom, by public speaking, through writing, or through individual instruction." It matters little what form this teaching takes. The "noblest calling of them all" pays dividends to teacher *and* student. It also helps you make many friends.

To best understand golf, teach it

It's instructive, I think, to reveal who offered me this advice. One adviser, the Canadian architect Stanley Thompson, was a genius and my mentor in course design. He created the world-renowned Capilano GC in Vancouver, Banff and Jasper Park in the Canadian Rockies, St. George's near Toronto, Highland Links in Nova Scotia, and scores of other inspired layouts. Visionary Lawrence S. Dickinson, the other adviser, was a professor at what is now the University of Massachusetts in Amherst. His educational work contributed immeasurably to finer lawns nationwide, not to mention the turf that golfers enjoy today on the glorious playing fields of the game.

Thompson and Dickinson both yearned to teach others. They taught me well. I've followed their advice and I've many friends to show for it.

Curt S. CULVER

President and CEO, MGIC Investment Corporation

Upon graduation from the University of Wisconsin, I was fortunate to find employment in Madison, Wisconsin, with a wonderful company, Verex. Even more fortunate for me was the fact that our CEO, Bruce Thomas, was an avid golfer.

During my high school and college years, I had amassed some recognition as a decent golfer in the Madison area. As a result, Mr. Thomas (Mr. Thomas was a great CEO, but he had a West Point background and insisted on being called "Mister" rather than Bruce) was aware of my golfing abilities. And like all CEOs, he was extremely competitive, which worked out to my benefit. Why? Two reasons. First, he loved to play golf with customers, and second, he loved to win, especially against better players (me).

So, it wasn't long after joining Verex that I was regularly joining Mr. Thomas and customers for weekly outings at his club. In fact, over the next three years, we probably played together thirty to forty times, with the customers enjoying our

Remember to play with respect

company and Mr. Thomas and I enjoying competing with each other.

It was at one of these later outings that I made an error in judgment. We had just played a terrific round of golf with fun customers and all of us had played well, especially

Mr. Thomas. So, over a few of Milwaukee's finest, we discussed the day's events. As a young buck, I probably had a couple more beers than the rest, which clouded my thought process somewhat. In fact, I got so carried away in describing a beautiful seven iron Mr. Thomas had hit (he one-hopped it into the hole for an eagle 2) that I blurted out, "That was one of the best shots I ever saw you hit, Bruce." As soon as the "Bruce" slipped out, I knew I was on thin ice, but mind you this was after having come to know this gentleman over three years and through multiple rounds of golf. However, it didn't matter. As soon as it slipped out, all chatter stopped, and he solemnly looked at me and said, "Curt, it's Mister Thomas."

Trust me, to this day, he is still Mr. Thomas and will always be Mr. Thomas. And while I have fun telling this story (and can still visualize it as if it were yesterday), the real point is the importance of golf to a business career. Here I was, a young person fresh out of graduate school, and I was playing golf with the CEO and our best customers. Clearly, this created an advantage for me relative to my career and, in a small way, helped prepare me for my role as CEO of MGIC. And, in case you're wondering, golf continues to be an important part of my career, but I insist on being called Curt.

Brian CURLEY

Principal, Schmidt-Curley Golf Design
(three of the firm's courses have garnered top 100
status from Golfweek*)*

I was fortunate to begin my career working alongside Pete Dye, one of the most influential golf architects in the profession's history. While Pete's bold designs bucked traditional sensibilities and established him as an artist, those of us around him learned not only his philosophy on design and strategy, but also his quirky, whimsical, offbeat views on life in general. Pete is very much his own man and is little concerned with how he is perceived. He speaks his mind and lets others deal with it. While many people act this way, few combine it with a genuine, warm, endearing personality that wins you over and makes you say, "Yes," despite your instinct to say, "No."

Combining his bold vision with a low tolerance for lost time, Pete always insisted on dealing with main decision makers. "Go to the top dog," he told me, advising never to waste time and effort on middlemen.

Go straight to the top

This advice has helped me establish great relationships with many "top dogs," most notably Dr. David Chu, the man behind the massive Mission Hills Golf Club in China, where our strong relationship led to my designing eight of his ten golf courses, helping to create the largest golf complex in the world.

Jim ENGH

Architect (designs include The Golf Club at Redlands Mesa, Grand Junction, Colorado; Sanctuary Golf Course, Sedalia, Colorado; Fossil Trace Golf Club, Golden, Colorado)

I was a young man, just a few years out of college, with some golf course design and construction experience. Living in Europe, I was designing courses for Bernard Langer and several other notable players. One of my first projects with Langer was in Austria for a man named Charlie Kahr, who happened to be the head coach for the Austrian National Ski Team. He was a man revered throughout his entire country.

As can be the case with many young people in a position of newfound responsibility, I tended to try and overcome my youth and inexperience by holding firm positions and fearing that compromise was a sign of weakness. On one occasion while debating with Charlie about the best type of machinery available for shaping the course, Charlie stated in German, "*Sie müssen nicht alle Antworten wissen.*" Seeing my puzzled look he said, "Jim, it's okay to not have all of the answers." I humbly nodded to Charlie my recognition that I had not yet earned my stripes to act in such a brash manner.

Don't be afraid to ask for help

Upon reflection, I understood what he was teaching me, and with that principle well in place I became much better at accepting the views of others. This was a very important lesson for a young man who was at the time working in five different countries. That single experience also changed my mind in how I view and appreciate many different kinds of golfing experiences. It ultimately made me much better at my profession.

Mark FASCIANO

CEO, FatWire Software

Ten years ago, I first played golf with my father-in-law, Tom Mitchell, at the links course at the Carnegie Club Skibo Castle in Dornoch, Scotland. I was fresh out of grad school and had just started my first software company, FatWire Software. Everything was new—shareholders agreements, producing financial statements, landing our first big customers—particularly for a guy who just traded in his hightops for oxfords. With so much to pick up, I tried to learn everything by the book, and this included golf.

To prepare for golf at Skibo with Tom, I took a bank of lessons: grip, stance, swing. I spent more on lessons and gear than I spent on food for a year as a single grad student. My head was filled with tips. Left arm straight. Head down. Accelerate the clubface through the swing. And then came the big day.

My wife and I flew out to Inverness and took a car to Skibo. We all met for dinner in the Carnegie Club dining room. Tom has always been a natural athlete: captain of his college football team, a marathon runner. His daughters, including my wife, were also college athletes.

Play by feel, not by the book

We played the next day. It was a complete disaster. Now, I'm not that bad of an athlete, and I'm competitive to a fault, but you couldn't tell that day. I tried to follow every lesson I'd learned, but nothing worked. Over 100 for the game. The running joke was to blame the wind whipping off Dornoch Firth, but it didn't affect Tom's game. He was gracious through the day, dodging the divots I sent flying in every direction, and tried to cheer me up. He told me, "We're going to fix your game."

Over a glass of Lagavulin, he tried to get me to relax—golf is only a game. After dinner we went for a walk. It was a dark, moonless night, and we walked back to the links course. He had the short clubs and putters brought out to the first hole. We played the hole in almost complete darkness. I would swing at a ball I could hardly see and connect and have no idea where the ball went. But we would walk down only to stumble on the ball in the middle of the fairway. No balls lost. When we reached the green, I putted. It was ridiculous; it was so dark I could only hear the flag forty feet away. But I putted anyway, relying completely on feel, and after a few seconds heard the sound of the ball dropping in the cup. I did what I couldn't do during the light of day. I had parred the hole in darkness.

I took that lesson back with me to work. I still read my books, but when it's time to play, I leave the books on the shelf and let instinct take over.

Dana GARMANY

Founder, Chairman, and CEO, Troon Golf

Although I had epiphanies early in my playing career, for great golf advice that had a long-lasting effect on me I can only refer to business advice.

In the early days of Troon Golf, I had this idea to use the model of the hotel industry to build a golf company. When I started, people knew it as Dana Garmany's company. I was so naive that I thought it was really cool to have my name on all the contracts and documents.

Surround yourself with quality people

Rick Kleeman, senior managing director of Starwood Capital, who is on our board and who understands how to build company value, said to me: "Do you think one day you might not want to work anymore? Do you think you might want to eventually sell the company?" His point was that I needed to build a company that would survive me, a company built for fifty years, not just three or four.

This was advice that I took to heart early on. I started to realize that this company needed to be about more than me, and I built Troon Golf around great people, on the principle of enterprise value. Basically, Rick was telling me: "Hey, dummy, unless you want to work until you're ninety, you better develop another plan."

John J. GLOZEK Jr.

Publisher, Long Island Golfer Magazine

The best golf advice I ever received was not actually advice, it was a question. I had been working at one of Long Island's largest employers for about six months. I eventually wound up working there for about six years. As I walked the hallways, went to meetings, and sat in the cafeteria, one subject kept coming up time and time again—golf.

It was discussed in meetings: "Did you see that shot Tiger hit this weekend?" and "Is it even possible to get a tee time at the Bethpage Black Course?" Golf seemed to be the topic everywhere in the workplace. One day it hit me: If I was going to move up the corporate ladder, all I had to do was go play golf. A few weeks later, while I was on the phone, my boss came over to my cubicle and said, "We need a fourth for Thursday. Do you play golf?" Honestly, I was in such shock, I almost didn't know what he meant. I mean, what's a fourth anyway? I took the phone away from my ear and said, "Sure, that would be great." My next call was to my dad (who has played golf most of his life). I told him, "Dad, I need to borrow your golf clubs. I just told my boss I play golf." The truth was that I don't think I had hit a golf ball in almost twenty years. My dad's response was "You said what?"

"Yeah, I need to borrow your golf clubs on Thursday. I told my boss I play golf," I replied. Well, Thursday came and went—I think I shot a 119. After a few more rounds under my belt (mind you, some of them were in the middle of the workday), I decided it was time to get my own set of clubs. I joined the corporate league and played a couple of times a week. And after starting a regional golf magazine, I even interviewed the CEO of the company. Fifteen years later, after hundreds of rounds on some of the best golf courses anywhere, I reflect on that day when my boss came to me and said, "Do you play golf?"

Golf is good for business

Business golf should be a part of everyone's business plan.

Chris HAACK

Head Coach, Men's Golf, University of Georgia

I had spent sixteen years working for the American Junior Golf Association (AJGA) in various positions (tournament director, director of operations, foundation director, and assistant executive director), but never ascending to the top position of executive director.

The head men's golf coaching position at the University of Georgia had just become available due to a coach's retiring and the school search committee approached me about taking the position.

Having spent all of my adult life out of college with the AJGA, I was very comfortable and secure with my job position in the organization. However, I felt I needed to call and talk about the opportunity presented to me with one of our board members, CEO and president of Titleist, Wally Uihlein. As an industry leader in golf, I sought his counsel on what I should do.

Wally gave me this advice: "You have done a great job at the AJGA, but the current executive director isn't going anywhere anytime soon. Sometimes in life you only get one chance to be the captain of your own ship, and that is when you find out who you are and what you are made of." So, I made the move!

Take control of your own destiny

That was 1996. In my second year, we won the SEC championship and in 1999, we won the NCAA championship. I have since added three more SEC championships and my current team is ranked first. I made the right move, but I have Wally's advice to thank for pushing me out of the nest!

Jeff HARP

President, Trinity Bank

I was fortunate enough to be able to play at Augusta several years ago. My caddy was a philosopher who carried a golf bag. He was fond of saying, "Golf is like business." Here are a few of the quotes that I remember (this was done with tongue in cheek—I laughed the whole way around).

Business Lesson—Don't Blame Others

> Golfer: "You are the worst caddy in the world."
> Caddy: "I don't think so. That would be too much of a coincidence."

Business Lesson—Don't Complain About Business Conditions

> Golfer: "This is the worst course I've ever played on."
> Caddy: "This isn't the golf course. We left that some time back."

Business Lesson—Face Reality

> Golfer: "This can't be my ball; it's too old."
> Caddy: "It's been a long time since we teed off."

Bill KUBLY

CEO, Landscapes Unlimited
(designed more than four hundred golf courses,
including Sand Hills in Nebraska, acclaimed as the
best course built since 1960, and Sutton Bay Club in
South Dakota, declared Best New Private Course
for 2004 by Golf Digest)

Being humble was my greatest lesson, and I learned it from Bill Coore and Ben Crenshaw, who displayed this attribute by their actions and words. When they designed Sand Hills, they weren't braggadocios but gave credit where it was due, saying the golf course was designed by the good Lord and they had simply discovered it.

Since then, when we've been credited with building Sand Hills, I've always clarified it as a great job done by the Lord. I feel the same way about Sutton Bay, where we've been given credit for building this extraordinary golf course. I always say, "The good Lord built it."

This lesson—be humble—is so true, whether it concerns your job, or life in general.

E. Stanley O'NEAL

Chairman and CEO, Merrill Lynch

When I decided to take up golf I was forty-five years old and had never been on a golf course. I didn't own a set of clubs and didn't belong to any clubs where I could play. For someone who felt reasonably accomplished professionally, trying to learn to play at this stage of my life was daunting, especially when it came to playing with clients and Merrill Lynch colleagues, all of whom seemed, in contrast to me, to be good or very good golfers.

So, the best advice I ever got was this: no one cares about *your* golf game because they're completely focused on their own, as long as you don't hold up the round—that is, pick up if you're out of the hole. In this way, I was able to play with a lot of great golfers and in many instances get to know them for the first time in ways that would have been impossible otherwise. And I'm the better person for it.

Jack PURCELL

Owner and Publisher, Links *Magazine*

The best golf advice I ever received—which was given to me by a number of very smart publishing executives—was that if I was to get into the very competitive golf magazine business, the only way to be successful in the long term was to develop a very distinctive editorial niche that subscribers and advertisers couldn't get from existing magazines. Many golf magazines have come and gone in the past ten years, while *Links* has prospered because we have never written about instruction and have always targeted the very affluent, passionate golfing executive, who is more interested in lifestyle (travel, resorts, real estate, etc.) than in reading about instruction.

Lee SCOTT

President and CEO, Wal-Mart Stores, Inc.

If you play fast, you will be invited to play regardless of how high your handicap.

Steve SMYERS

Architect (designs include Wolf Run Golf Club in Zionsville, Indiana; Old Memorial Golf Club in Tampa, Florida; and Southern Dunes Golf & Country Club in Haines City, Florida; latest design was a complete reconstruction of Isleworth Golf Club in Florida, the home of Tiger Woods and a dozen other PGA Tour professionals)

The best advice for my design business came from my wife, Sherrin, and my associate, Patrick Andrews. Sherrin told me not to be influenced by publications or critics, but to trust my heart and instincts, and just let the golf course design happen.

"You know what a good golf course is," she said. "Just go and do it and don't worry about it."

Don't be overwhelmed by technical details

Once when Patrick and I were walking a property for which I was having trouble figuring out the routing, he said, "Steve, don't worry about the technical components. Once you read the land and understand what it has to say, everything will work into place, and the golf course will have a more natural feeling and last through the ages."

The best golfing advice came from Buster Bishop, my coach at the University of Florida.

He said, "If you slice it into the trees, go in there and slice it back out." He was basically saying, "Go play golf and no matter what it takes, get it in the hole."

Bill STAVROPOULOS

Chairman, Dow Chemical Company

Play fast.

Think about your next shot as you walk to the ball, not when you're standing over it. In business, it's the difference between formulating a strategy and implementing a strategy—planning and executing.

Also, replace your divots, and think about the people who care for the course and who play on it. In industry, that translates to caring about the environment—thinking about the generations after you.

Ty VOTAW

Commissioner, LPGA

I receive a lot of advice about how to do my job as commissioner of the LPGA. Some I solicit, but the vast majority comes to me unsolicited. One of the best pieces of unsolicited advice came to me while I was on the golf course.

It was during a pro-am, very early in my tenure as LPGA commissioner. One of the people in my group that day was the CEO of a local hospital that was the charitable beneficiary of the tournament. Because it was one of my first pro-ams as commissioner, I was a little nervous and more than a little self-conscious about the quality of my game (I have a 20 handicap). After about six holes, the CEO put his arm around me as we were walking down the fairway and said, "You know, Ty, the surgeons in my hospital often tell me that it isn't necessary for me to be a great surgeon in order for me to be a great hospital administrator. After six holes, I can tell you don't have to be a good golfer to be an excellent commissioner."

Be the best at what you do

From that moment on, I had a better perspective about the relationship between my job and my skills as a golfer. In fact, it helped me become more at ease in both settings and made me appreciate the benefits of playing "customer golf"—because when I play with a customer, the customer usually wins.

Suzanne WOO

Founder and President, BizGolf Dynamics
Author, On Course for Business

While working as a junior attorney in a San Francisco law firm, I received some business advice that is ultimately the best golf advice I've ever gotten. "Not every client is a good client," the partner shared as we were discussing whether the firm would take on a matter. He meant some clients can never be satisfied—regardless of the outcome, they have unreasonable expectations that can't be diminished.

As I played more golf, I realized that golf is the most effective tool to help determine the true character and personality of a person. Did he cheat? Did she have unreasonable expectations? Would I want to play golf with that person again, let alone do business with him or her? Use golf to cut your losses or make lots of money by working with people you know, like, and trust.

Summation of the advice: "Golf tells no lies."

Golf
301

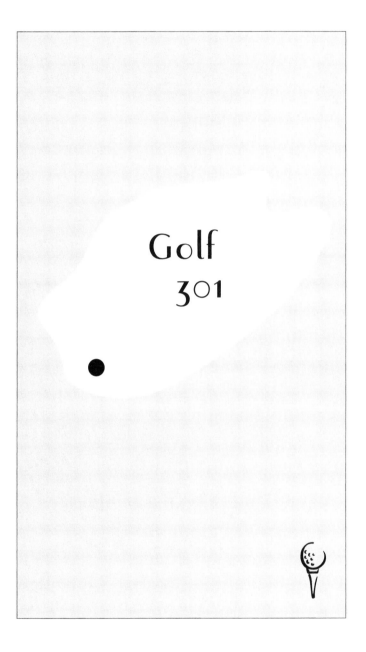

Linda COHN

Anchor, ESPN

The best golf advice I ever received helped me break 90 for the first time two years ago.

I was playing in the pro-am in the event formerly known as the GHO in Cromwell, Connecticut (it's now called the Buick).

The PGA player in my group was Joey Sindelar. He really took an interest in my game. Joey noticed that when I was around the green I automatically would take out one of my wedges, a sand or pitching, in order to make the perfect chip shot. The thing is that I rarely made that perfect chip shot using a wedge. That's when Joey gave me this advice:

Use your putter more

Unless you're in rough, use your putter! Why? Because you have more control over your putter. Even if you mishit, you'll still end up in the right neighborhood. The ball usually ends up *on* the green, not *over* it or back at your feet.

It's the advice I like to call "Don't risk a *wedgie*." If you do, it not only can cause you discomfort, but by the end of the day, you will be in pain—especially when you look at your final score.

Denton A. COOLEY

President and Surgeon in Chief, Texas Heart Institute

Keep the ball in the fairway when the choice is a bunker on the right side and a pond on the left. Hitting the ball out of sand is difficult, but it's impossible out of water.

Don't blame poor shots on the equipment. The fault is not with the arrow, but with the Indian.

Golf is a four-letter word—other words of four letters were already taken and used frequently on the course.

Brian A. CROWELL

PGA Instructor
Head Golf Professional, Leewood Golf Club,
Eastchester, New York

"Play the ball as it lies!"

So many golfers are tempted to improve the lie of their golf ball. I see players who cannot resist "fluffing" their ball into a nice position before making a swing. They play "winter rules" whenever they like, they play "hurricane rules" (which allow them to move leaves and sticks in bunkers), they allow each other to "roll the ball over" if it's in the fairway, and so on. These practices make a golfer weak—and I haven't even mentioned "gimme putts" and "mulligans"!

I urge golfers at every level of ability to be true to themselves and to this great game.

If your ball comes to rest in a divot, don't roll it out of the divot before you swing—play it as it lies! If your ball is in a footprint in the bunker, play it as it lies!

If your ball is sitting on hardpan or buried in the rough, play it as it lies! Get used to playing these shots, and you will become a much stronger player! In fact, if such lies scare you, then I encourage you to practice from such conditions. And please refuse gimmes, and don't take mulligans. Just play your best and enter your score! I guarantee you will become a better player.

If you want to get better, stop cheating

Glenn DECK

PGA Instructor
Director of Instruction, Pelican Hill Golf Academy

Scottish golfer pros knew what they were talking about 200 years ago. They focused on simple fundamentals:

SETUP: Have good posture and aim so that you're ready to swing the club.

BACKSWING: Make sure that your back is turned to the target, a good pivot turning back and not a lift.

DOWNSWING: Make sure that your hands and arms swing the club down to the ball instead of an around swing.

SAME MOVEMENT: Learn one swing that works for your full swing, sand shots, pitch shots, and chip shots.

When hitting the driver, don't focus on maximum distance

The driver is the hardest club to hit because we all try to hit as far as John Daly, thus losing our tempo and proper sequence of motion. All our other clubs have a set distance parameter that you want to hit, which helps promote your tempo and sequence. Not the driver. Learn to swing your driver like your wedge or seven iron; focus on direction and how solid you hit it, not maximum distance. You'll benefit by hitting your driver straighter and more consistently.

Ann Meyers DRYSDALE

Basketball Hall of Fame
First Woman to Play in the Bob Hope Classic and
on the Celebrity Players Tour

I was the first female Hall of Famer to play in the Don Drysdale Hall of Fame Golf Classic, and my handicap was as low as a 6. The best score I had was a 76 with Don at the Club at Morningside in Rancho Mirage, California.

Tom Watson once gave me a great piece of advice. His suggestion to those who don't play on a professional level was that they should probably take one more club than they think they should. That has helped me out.

Watson also said amateurs think they can get there with the clubs the pros use. They think they can. But you have to put your ego in check. That's the mental aspect of not letting your ego get in the way. You hit a nine iron when you should have been using an eight or a seven. The guy that taught me was Lou Rosanova. He just passed away a year ago. I picked up the game with Don. I really didn't play, but when I met Donnie, he got me playing the game.

> **Don't bring your ego onto the course**

It was 1984 when I really began to take it seriously. I got down to a 6 in two or three weeks. I understood the game because of the guy I was working with, Lou. He was originally from Chicago, and a lot of the senior guys know who he was. He didn't play in the pros, but he was one of those guys who played for money.

Lou said, "It doesn't matter if you miss left, right, long or short. Ten yards is ten yards."

Mentally, the bottom line is you have to hit the shot. People are like "Oh, no, I'm over here." He said, "If you miss it, you miss it." You gotta play the hole, you gotta play the game. He really worked on me mentally.

I played golf one time with Willie Mosconi. He was uncanny around the greens. It was like setting up your next shot in pool.

That's what Lou taught me. Whatever the shot, you set it up. He really prepared me for the mental game. That was really the key to understanding to play short and how to approach every shot.

Rod GILBERT

New York Rangers, 1960–1978
Hockey Hall of Fame

For many, many years, I played in the Crosby in North Carolina at Bermuda Run.

One time, I was teamed up with Lou Holtz, the former coach at Notre Dame. He's quite an inspirational guy. After the fifteenth hole on a par 3 where I made a 9, I asked him why I was playing so bad. What was I doing wrong?

If you don't play it for a living, golf is only a game

He said, "I have one piece of advice for you. As a hockey player, you have really good motion and eye-hand coordination. But you might be too worried about this game. After this tournament, you should take a couple of weeks off and ignore golf when you get back to New York. And, after the two weeks, I suggest you quit the game." Can you imagine that? I listened to this for, like, five minutes as he's giving me this speech about the game and then he says, "Quit; you're taking this too seriously."

This is when I realized it was only a game and I wasn't making a living out of it. That's when I started to enjoy it for whatever it offers you.

Chuck HOGAN

Golf Digest *Top 100 Teacher*
Author of Ten Instructional Books

In the course of my life and golf career, I've received good advice from extremely disparate sources. When I was about fourteen years old, a very good adult player had been watching me play. Observing my inappropriate behavior after hitting a bad shot he said, "Tell me just one way that getting upset, angry, and depressed about a golf shot is going to help you." Although he posed this as a question, the advice inherent in it was obvious even to me at the time.

Before that incident, which has stuck with me to this day, my mother once suggested that I imagine a red dot on the back of the golf ball and a blue dot in the middle of the clubface. "After you can connect those two dots nearly all the time, then add a yellow dot at the target," she said. This was very good technical advice that helped me tremendously.

If you don't worry about getting better, you will get better

Another time, I was playing with a fellow junior golfer who later went on to play the tour. During our round he said to me, "Every shot you save now is one less birdie you have to make on the back nine, or tomorrow." That really put in perspective for me both the nature of competitive golf and the idea about living in the present.

Finally, one of the best pieces of golf advice I ever came across was from Shivas Irons in Michael Murphy's book *Golf in the Kingdom.* The old golf pro said, "Fuck oor e'er gettin' bitter." For me, it took years and years for that piece of advice to sink in. Intellectually, I knew that the idea that I would like the game as soon as I got better is golf's catch-22, as well as the source of unending frustration. Nevertheless, Americans have a very hard time playing the game for the sake of pure play. Repeat it with me now: Fuck our ever getting better!

Dr. Michael HURDZAN

Principal, Hurdzan/Fry Golf Course Design (designs are ranked among the top one hundred modern courses by Golfweek *and in* Golf Digest's *Top 75 Public Courses)*

The best piece of golf advice I ever received came from my mom, who said, "There are two ways to be rich—one is to have a lot of money, and the other is to have simple needs." That was literally a life-altering statement, for it shaped and continues to shape my personal and professional way of thinking, and is even reflected in my golf-course design philosophy.

Since I live my life in this fashion, I am always doing cost-to-benefit ratios to determine the true value of something. This philosophy leads me to build golf courses at as low a cost as possible while still making them fun to play and easy to maintain. I believe that the most important part of designing a golf course is a skillful routing of golf holes to minimize all phases of construction. We strive to limit site disturbance and to keep the topsoil in place, treating it as gently as a farmer would. Earth moving is a last resort. We value irrigation water as a precious resource that should be used as sparingly as possible to sustain healthy plant growth.

Become a good judge of a course's natural conditions

This "one with nature" philosophy carries over to playing golf, too, in that hazards are meant to be penal and not manicured, that hitting a driver off every par 4 and 5 tee is not always the intelligent play, and that greens should be smooth but not necessarily fast. A simple golf course requires more thoughtful shot making because such a golf course is not maintained from fence line to fence line just to look pretty, and hence can produce quirky conditions. Golfers must become better judges of changing conditions of firmness as the soils naturally move from wet to dry or from season to season. The best player is the one who understands these natural dynamics and shows the best course management skills, the one who is able to invent and not just play golf shots, and the one who can deal with unexpected challenges. This is "true golf" as it was meant to be played, and all this fun can be had for a fraction of the cost required to build and maintain a golf course that is always green and boringly predictable. As a designer, I find that it is more gratifying to produce a wonderful, fun golf course that incorporates characteristic features of the site than it is to ignore them and manufacture artificial ones at a much higher cost. I have been fortunate to travel and play golf around the world, not as a celebrity on immaculate, posh golf courses, but as an unknown on tracks where the locals play. Some of the courses have been historic but simple venues like the West Course at North Berwick, Maine, or the twelve-hole Skiskine course on the Scottish Isle of Arran. Others have been cow pasture golf courses like Krambach, north of Sydney, Australia, sand green golf courses in Alaska, or other unknown, homemade courses. Some of these anonymous golf courses charged a few dollars to play, but in all cases I thoroughly enjoyed my day of golf, and had money left over to buy a few beers in a local pub with some new golfing friends that I met that day—along with some priceless memories. I am a very rich man because I have simple needs, and it was all because someone gave me some wonderful advice for life and golf.

Ferguson JENKINS

National Baseball Hall of Fame

Grip it and rip it. Keep it in the short grass, and if you can't play the lie, you're gonna be in trouble.

Raymond Floyd and Kenny Still used to be real good friends of the Chicago Cubs. So every time they would show up, being that they were friends of a lot of players on the team like Ron Santo, Billy Williams, and myself, it was always good to keep your ear close to how they were describing things and how they were doing things. When Raymond Floyd was winning big tournaments, they weren't worth like a million dollars. He was winning them for $5,000 and $6,000. He used that Ram Zebra putter, and I have been using it for the last fifteen years. It's a good mallet putter, and I feel comfortable putting with it.

Cathy MacPHERSON

Golf for Women *Magazine Top 50 Teacher*

We've all had the experience of what I call "Doing the Math" while playing a round of golf. At some point during the round we start to add things up. This usually occurs after a few less than desirable holes, and the numbers on the scorecard start to resemble numbers given out in gymnastics competitions (rounded up, of course). The "Doing the Math" stage is immediately followed by the "Projection Stage": "If I just par the next two holes and make a birdie on the back, I'll have a decent score." This cycle continues until we reach the fifteenth hole. At this point we realize there is no possible way to salvage the round and achieve that "decent score" we were hoping for over the eighteen holes of play. While finishing the last few holes of the round, we start to recap and enter the final "If Only" stage: "If only the wind hadn't picked up and knocked the ball into the hazard . . . If only that drive on number six hadn't gone into the woods, if only that fifteen footer on three fell in . . ." The decent score continued to be elusive until this scorecard management strategy was introduced.

The secret to the success of scoring was moving away from the mind-set of a single round of golf consisting of eighteen holes to six rounds of golf each consisting of three holes. The front side now had three rounds of golf, and the back side also had three rounds of golf. Now there was an opportunity to have a "decent round of golf" multiple times during the course of play. It took the pressure off of the total score and allowed the focus to shift in the direction of the shot at hand. You could stay in the present more easily.

Stop doing the math on the course

No more "Doing the Math." If a bad hole crept into a round, it was only one hole. There were many opportunities to regroup and start fresh. The next "new round" was about to begin. Instead of just one round of golf, you now had six. Everything became easier and more manageable. The pressure diminished, the enjoyment flourished, and the scores came down significantly. Golf was once again the best game in the world.

David MARR III

Host, The Golf Channel's Golf Central Updates *and* Grey Goose 19th Hole

Three things . . . one at a time.

I've had the good fortune of being exposed to some outstanding golfers and teachers. From Gene Sarazen to Ben Hogan to Paul Runyan to my father, each student of the game has his own unique approach to the swing. There are certain schools of thought and similarities from swing to swing, but the differences from golfer to golfer range from subtle to dramatic. With such a wide array of philosophies there is a temptation to sip from a variety of cups, but beware the swing hangover! Contradiction and confusion can prevail and render your game worse off than when you started. The best advice I ever received came to me from my father, and to him from one of the greatest golf instructors in history, 1948 Masters champion Claude Harmon. The advice is simple and pure— work on one thing at a time. Ingrain the new swing feature on the practice tee, and then test it

Focus on one new thing at a time

under pressure on the course. It is the only way to ensure that the foundation being built will last over time and support any future modifications. Trying too many changes at once will only undermine your efforts on each.

Two other quick tidbits I've picked up along the way hold true no matter what changes I make. The first is the

Nicklaus alignment key. Without proper alignment, a good swing is useless, and Jack's advice is the best I've heard in that regard. Stand behind the ball and pick out a target. Then pick a spot on the ground or blade of grass that is within a couple of feet of your ball and along the same target line. Take your stance, making sure your feet and body are parallel to the line created by your ball and that spot, and you will find yourself aligned properly to the target.

Another piece of worthy advice from my father helped my chipping by equating the stroke to an underhanded throw in force and mechanics. It immediately helped with distance control and motion. Swinging a sand wedge as hard as I would throw a ball underhanded to the hole always gives me a chance to get up and down. Also, as with an underhanded throw, a typical chip from a decent lie requires a fairly short backswing and a decent follow-through. Too many amateurs stab at the ball when chipping. While this might have worked once or twice in the past, the underhanded throwing motion is a better play on a percentage basis. In short, when chipping, try to mirror the pace and mechanics of an underhanded throw.

Jay MORRISH

*Architect (designs include Troon Golf & Country Club,
The Boulders North and South, Forest Highlands in
Arizona and the TPC course for the Byron Nelson
Tournament; Six of his designs have been listed as among
the top courses in the U.S., Britain, and/or the world)*

In the late 1960s, I worked for George Fazio, who had
been a great golfer and had won the Canadian Open and
the Crosby among other tournaments and had lost a U.S.
Open play-off to Ben Hogan. In the early 1960s, he began designing golf courses.

Over the last thirty years, I have received many, many golf
course design tips, 95 percent of
which I ignore. However, one
simple tip from George has
stayed with me. He told me:
"Never stand on a tee you
are building and look down the
fairway head on. Turn sideways and pretend you are addressing a ball. Then, look down the fairway from that
position. Unnoticed flaws will become quickly visible. For
instance, trees on the right side of the tee and slightly in
front of the tee may totally stop someone from drawing
the ball. You don't see this without addressing the ball."

He was dead on.

**Change your
perspective and see
a whole new course**

Brenden PAPPAS

PGA Tour Player

In the business of professional golf, we are in a constant state of flux. Our environment is ever changing: the golf courses, the weather, the people we play with, the different grasses used, and so on. When we are out on the course competing, we are faced with several variables that have to be observed, and adjustments for each have to be made prior to the execution of each shot. I refer to such things as wind direction and speed, the ground condition (is it hard or soft . . . will the club dig or bounce?), the elevation change, and the receptiveness of the green relative to the pin position. The important thing to know is there are only a few things in golf one can control.

> Be patient—
> you can't control
> everything

I learned this when I was about twelve years old. I have three older brothers, Craigen, Sean, and Deane, all of whom are accomplished golfers. We grew up in a small mining community in the northeast of South Africa, in a place called Phalaborwa. There wasn't much in the way of entertainment to keep a teenager's mind occupied, so our family turned to the Hans Merensky Hotel and Estate for something to do.

Our parents would drop us off at the club after school and we would play golf all day long. My dad, Leon, would come out after work and teach us the nuances of the game at least three times a week. He believed that kids shouldn't receive lessons beyond the fundamentals until after their mid-teens. He believed in letting the child develop a natural talent for the game. As I am the youngest of the four boys, I used to sit and watch my dad work on swing plane, weight shift, and transition with my brothers. The times that we spent on the range are some of the fondest memories from my childhood. I learned my first great life lesson on that range—to be patient. I was twelve years old and about three years away from getting the same lessons my brothers were. As I sat and watched my brothers and dad, I learned just about everything there is in my dad's knowledge base about the game. When I was older and ready to go one-on-one with my dad, I thought I wouldn't learn much. Boy, was I wrong!

My first lesson was about fundamentals: The grip, ball position, posture, and alignment. The old boring stuff, right? Wrong! That is when I learned something from my dad that I would never forget. He said, "The only things in golf you can control are the fundamentals: the grip, ball position, posture, and alignment. That is why the preshot routine is the most important part of golf."

Jim PETRALIA

Golf Digest *Top 50 Teacher*

In 1979, I was the head professional at Montecito Country Club in Santa Barbara, California. I had an eighteen-year-old bag room employee by the name of Steve Pate. I was playing in the California State Open and Steve was my caddy. I managed to win the championship, which was a pretty big deal for a club professional. Feeling pretty full of myself at the time, I asked Steve if he might have learned anything valuable from observing my glorious triumph. His reply was swift and to the point: *"You don't have to hit the ball worth a damn to win a golf tournament."*

I am not sure who was giving whom the advice, but Steve certainly learned something that week. He is a multiple winner on the PGA Tour, and a two-time Ryder Cup team member. I have been his coach/teacher since those days, and frankly, his remark would be good advice for everyone.

Nancy QUARCELINO

Golf Magazine *Top 100 Teacher*
Golf for Women *Magazine Top 50 Teacher*

When I was still thinking about playing golf competitively, I was trying to qualify for a local LPGA tournament, the Sara Lee Classic. The tournament was located at my home facility, the Hermitage Golf Course in Old Hickory, Tennessee. I was the director of golf at that time and still young enough to have aspirations of qualifying and winning at my home facility.

I had given some swing advice to Harry Taylor, who played on the PGA Tour and who is now the senior director of club design and tour promotion for Mizuno. I asked Harry to give me the best advice he could about playing competitively and what would complement my game. He gave me the following advice, which I now give to my students.

- You want 3s and 4s on your scorecard. Always go for pars on the par 3 and 4 holes, going for birdies only on the par 5s.
- If the flag is located on the left or right side of the green, shoot for the middle of the green. It is best to be putting, than to be trying to get up and down after missing the green from a short-edge pin placement.

> **Aim to have 3s and 4s on your scorecard**

- If the flag is in the middle of the green, place your approach shot below the flag position for the best run at the birdie putt.
- If you have missed the green, don't be upset at the outcome. The shot you missed was the approach shot to the green, not the next chip or pitch shot.

As a teacher of the game, giving a student this advice keeps them in the present game and not in the how to play a shot.

T. J. TOMASI

Golf Magazine *Top 100 Teacher*

In order to maximize your potential in golf, you must address four areas:

1. Your swing
2. Your fitness
3. How you run your brain
4. Your equipment

In one way or another, each skill is easily improved.

Your Swing

The tip: "You need to match your swing type to your body type."

Golf is hard because most golfers have a swing that doesn't fit them. If you're struggling with your game, *it's not your fault—you're just mismatched.*

Your Fitness

The tip: "Everything else being equal, the strongest machine wins."

Cut your gym time if you must, but add an increased dose of "driver time" to your practice sessions.

How to Run Your Brain

The tip: "For thirty seconds on each shot, you need the focus of a snake charmer."

In order to give yourself your best chance of success, you must learn to apply all of your resources to each and every shot you hit, both in practice and in play. You do this by observing a ritual for every shot. The logic behind the ritual is that because the universe is an orderly place, it can be controlled by adhering to certain principles, and you gain access to these principles by the ritual.

Practice a ritual before every shot

Your Equipment

The tip: "Sometimes it's the arrows and not the Indian."

To maximize your performance, you should fit your golf clubs and your golf ball to your own personal characteristics, such as swing speed, strength, and body type. In other words "get thee to a fitter," then "try before you buy."

Deb VANGELLOW

2002 LPGA Central Section Teacher of the Year
Golf *and* Golf Digest *Top Regional Teacher*
Golf for Women *Magazine Top 50 Teacher*

We have all heard it: the well-intentioned advice to "keep your head down." Keeping your head down in a static sense is an unnatural and tense position. This is because keeping your head down rigidly restricts the free swinging motion of your body through the ball. You could easily wind up hitting at the ball rather than swinging through it.

Instead, try to "watch the collision" of the clubhead and ball. This thought will help keep your spine angle constant and your eyeline and attention on the ball. When the weight shifts and the rotation of the body occurs, the right shoulder passing under your chin will help your head come up after impact so that you can follow the flight of the ball, getting to the optimal balanced finish position. Remember, impact occurs during the swing, not at the end of it. Let the ball get in the way of the swing by watching the collision, not by keeping your head down. We want to see that great shot after it is gone, not while we are hitting it.

Norm WESLEY

Chairman and CEO, Fortune Brands, Inc.

Like so many other players who love the game, I'm a very average golfer. We know that golf can be pretty hard to play, and we can use all the help we can get.

That's why the best golf advice I ever received is promoted by club professionals everywhere: Get clubs that fit you and your game. Golf isn't a one-size-fits-all sport. Players come in all shapes and sizes, and so do their swings.

When I first took up golf, I had good clubs but I hadn't taken the time to have them custom-fitted. Then, I became

CEO of Fortune Brands—the consumer products company behind such great brands as Titleist, FootJoy, and Cobra—and my golf perspective changed dramatically. I learned pretty quickly that there are so many variables that impact a club's performance: loft, lie, shaft flex, and shaft kick point, among others. An iron that is too upright, for example, can promote a shot right of target. A shaft that's too stiff isn't opti-

Get the right clubs

mized for low-swing-speed players. Many players select a driver with too little loft, depriving themselves of valuable distance. The variables can be dizzying, but the solution is simple: Most club professionals will take the time to fit any golfer to clubs optimized for his or her game. Let's face it, golf is difficult enough without having to play with the wrong equipment.

The first time I played with clubs that were custom-fitted, I could tell the difference right away. Same player, better results. Shots went farther. Shots went straighter. And I'll even admit to eventually making a hole in one—at Pebble Beach.

Jerry WEST

General Manager, Memphis Grizzlies
Los Angeles Lakers, 1960–1974
Basketball Hall of Fame
Selected as One of the 50 Greatest Players in
NBA History

Oh boy, that's a tough one.

Probably the best golf advice that I think I ever received was to just not go out to the driving range and hit golf balls all the time but spend more of my time around the greens and bunkers, practicing twenty-five, thirty-yard shots, fifty-yard shots.

Focus on your short game

I think that for the person who gets to the point of becoming a competent golfer—and I'm talking about a single-digit handicap—that's the best advice of all.

If you watch professionals practice, they practice certain things that amateurs are not capable of doing. But the one thing they all realize, and maybe I realized when I was a decent player, was that the more time I spent around the green—chipping, pitching, trying different kinds of shots, different kinds of clubs from different kinds of lies—was time well spent. I learned more from that maybe than any lesson that I've ever taken.

When I was a decent player, an awful lot of my time was spent on the putting green. I didn't practice ten- or fifteen-foot putts. I always practiced putts from forty feet, fifty feet, and also about three feet. I became a good putter.

I had a routine when I played golf on a regular basis. I went out on the driving range and hit balls for four hours until I found out that where I was missing most of my shots, and where I was missing an opportunity to score, was from around the green and close to the green, particularly bunkers. You find out that those shots are not hard, but you need a method for doing it.

Frankly, you can get those methods out of any golf book. They're not hard, but most people don't want to do that. They want to see how far they can hit the ball, and they want to see the ball go in the air, so they have little or no patience for that part of the game. That, to me, is ultimately the most important part of the game.

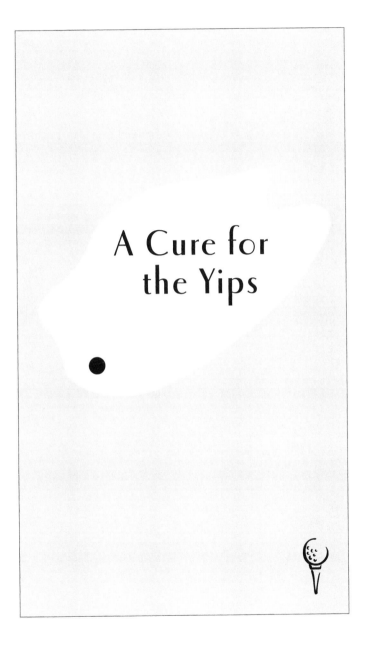

A Cure for
the Yips

Patricia BAXTER-JOHNSON

LPGA Tour Player

The 2005 season will be my sixth year playing on the LPGA Tour. I live in Lake Worth, Florida, and represent the Breakers in Palm Beach, Florida. Of all sources, I received this advice from Rick Wynn, a caddy who is a great observer of the game and very accomplished. He has caddied for many PGA Tour, PGA Senior Tour, and LPGA Tour players. I have worked with numerous top-fifty teaching instructors, and this is one of the best stroke-saving pieces of advice I have ever received.

My first year on the LPGA Tour, most places we played had been in a drought and everything was playing hard and fast. I was always a good short putter and loved fast greens, but I was having trouble with my focus on six-to-ten-foot putts. I was too result oriented and worrying if I had made the putt before I was even able to put a good stroke on the ball. I was told to narrow my focus by concentrating on rolling the ball down my line. I only needed to focus on the starting line of my putt and getting the

Get the ball rolling down the line

ball rolling down that line. That would give me the best chance to make the putt and keep me from guiding the ball toward the hole. It really helped me stay in the putt longer and make a good stroke. Once I put that thought in my putting routine, I made myself stick to it no matter what, and it started to pay off. I really got my mind more into the putt instead of into the results and worrying about where the hole was. When I play in pro-ams, I see so many amateurs trying to stroke and guide their putt to the hole instead of on the line they have picked. Ninety percent of the time it's not their stroke that is making them miss; it's because they are too result oriented and simply need to make a good stroke on the line of the putt they have picked out.

Drill: Put a chalk line down about six feet from the hole, hit putts focusing on the first foot of your chalk line only, and roll the ball on that starting line. Don't look up at the hole at all, especially with your peripheral vision; just focus on the first foot where you start your putts.

Beverly FERGUSSON

Golf for Women *Magazine Top 50 Teacher*

"Beverly, the hole is not over when you arrive on the green . . . you still have to putt and get it in the hole!"

As a teenager growing up and playing golf at Starmount Country Club in Greensboro, North Carolina, I played a lot of golf. I worked so hard at keeping the ball in play, out of the woods, chipping it by the hole and having to chip again, that once I was on the green, I thought my work was over! My mind started wandering to the next tee shot before I had putted. I loved the tee shot. I was tall, strong, and could hit it a long way. Putting was boring and chipping was dreaded! But for me to enjoy this game more,

I had to change my thinking! One day I was playing with my mother and a friend of hers, Marge Burns. Marge was the club champion, a North Carolina state champion, a North Carolina Golf Hall of Fame Member, and later a noted LPGA Teaching Professional. She was my idol. When she spoke those words to me in her soft but firm and direct manner, I listened. It woke me up as to what part of the game was most important in scoring better and actually having more fun. She taught me to chip and putt! Marge is still my idol, and that was forty-two years ago.

Marty FLECKMAN

Former PGA Tour Player

I asked Byron Nelson, "What do you think is the most important shot in golf?"

He said, "A putt from six feet and under."

I asked him why, and he said, "Because if you miss a drive, you can recover with a good second shot. If you miss your second shot, you can recover with a wedge or a pitch or a chip. If you miss a short putt, there's no recovering."

Byron worked with my game from about 1964 to 1974. We had a close relationship and I got lots of great information. He was a great role model.

Jerry FOLTZ

Reporter, The Golf Channel

When I was young, my teacher at Las Vegas Muni was a gentleman named Jerry Belt. While on the putting green one day I was talking about getting a long putt close, and he said to me, "You know, the hole is the same size from here as it is from three feet. Just try to make it from here, and at worst you'll be close." The moral of the story—the easiest way to two-putt is to try to one-putt. It was a lesson that stayed with me to this day. If it wasn't for my ability to putt, my dubiously underachieving career would have been even more obscure.

John FOUGHT

Architect (four courses ranked among the top
one hundred modern designs by Golfweek)
Two PGA Tour Titles
1977 U.S. Amateur Champion

Many things are curious to a young golf course architect as he begins his career. One of the first things I did when entering this field was to read design literature from the architects of the "Golden Age"—those who worked in the twenty-five-year period beginning in 1910.

Through my amateur and professional playing career, I had played many of the great courses of this era, including Augusta National, Pebble Beach, San Francisco Golf Club, Shinnecock, Pinehurst Number 2, and so on. My desire was to discover the secrets from those who designed such interesting golf courses. One of the key elements consistent in these masterpieces was putting surfaces. Greens are much of what makes these courses what they are—great and, most of all, timeless. Charles Blair McDonald, the first U.S. Amateur champion and an important design aficionado of the early years, said, "Putting greens to a golf course are what the face is to a portrait." That is as true today as it was when golf was initially being developed in America. With this in mind, I focused on fine-tuning my design for greens. On several of my early design projects, I endeavored to be precise with my sketches, hoping that the contractor would build my ideas exactly as I had drawn them. A funny thing happened— they did build them exactly as I drew them . . . and I was disappointed. I had been so perfectly precise with my contour lines, I couldn't help but wonder what had gone wrong.

It was then I came across a pearl of wisdom from one of the masters, Dr. Alister MacKenzie. When one of his golf course contractors was asked how he had achieved such wonderful movements in his newly constructed putting surfaces, MacKenzie said that "it was perfectly easy; he simply employed the biggest fool in the village and told him to make them flat." While this seemed a bit silly, it got me to thinking about the process I had been utilizing to design and build my greens. In a roundabout way, this approach made me

Get back to basics

rethink my method for building greens. I needed to go back to the basics. I discovered what I really wanted in my greens was soft, interesting contours that flowed naturally. After carefully studying my approach, I discovered that my method of carving out the greens cavity (for USGA specifications) during the initial construction process left me with disappointing results. My greens had become too geometric and static. So I resolved to design my greens in concept on paper first, and then finalize all the fine contours on the green on site by building all final grades first and then digging the well to conform to my finished grades. I am now able to achieve the results I am seeking—soft, natural contours.

With that small bit of thought provoking advice from an architect who had been dead for nearly sixty-five years, I gleaned some real value. With a small change in my method of construction, I was able to create wonderful interesting greens.

Clark GILLIES

New York Islanders/Buffalo Sabres, 1974–1988
Hockey Hall of Fame

We all have our own method of driving the ball, but putting is something else.

Basically, a guy once told me that it all has to do with the dominant eye. You figure out which eye is your dominant eye. And make sure that you focus on the ball with that eye. With putting, it takes very little to go wrong. If your eyes start to move, your head moves with your eyes; and if your head moves, your body moves. So it all really begins with the eyes. If the eyes can stay very quiet and very focused on the ball, very little other movement will take place. I think that, probably more than anything, is important.

Mark GRODY

President, Corporategolf.com
Author, Corporate Golf: How to Play the Game
for Business Success

To say that the best golf advice I ever received helped my putting is like saying that Beethoven was a piano player! Of course Beethoven played the piano, but he was so much more than that; and the best golf tip I got didn't just "help" my putting, it consistently knocked a couple of strokes off my game.

My tip came from Mike Clifford, director of golf at the Lakes Country Club where I live in Palm Desert, California. Mike taught me his "short putt drill," and the concept is so simple it's scary! It makes the cup look like the size of a manhole in the street.

Here's the idea: First, find a flat area on the practice putting green. Then imagine the cup split into thirds—the right third, the center third, and the left third.

From twelve inches and no more, make the putt twice in the right third, then twice in the left third. Then back up to twenty-four inches and do the same. You will find that you have to roll the ball very softly to the left or right third or the ball will lip out.

Visualize a bigger cup

Move back to thirty-six inches and start rolling the ball into the center third. Then keep moving back twelve inches with each two putts. You may find that you are ten feet away from the hole before you miss a putt. You will find that your speed is so good that even when you miss the center third, many putts will still fall in.

When you play your next round of golf, all you need to do is get within three feet of the hole, and all putts from that distance will seem like gimmes.

Try it the next time you're at the practice putting green.

Jay HILL

PGA Instructor

The best golf advice I ever received was a putting tip from a college classmate at Furman University, Brad Faxon. Brad is a highly regarded putter and is considered by many to be the best putter to have ever played professional golf. Bobby Locke, Ben Crenshaw, and Tiger Woods are the only other players in the history of the game that have a similar reputation.

One significant piece of putting advice that Brad gave me was that all of one's missed putts must miss on the high side of the hole. You will never become a good putter until all of your misses are on the high side. A breaking putt has zero chance of going in if the target line is below the hole. Conversely,

If you're going to miss, miss on the high side

no matter what the pace, a putt still has a chance of going in if the line is at least on the high side of the hole. Great advice that works wonders!

But the best advice that Brad ever gave me was in the form of a written message on a Scotty Cameron head cover that said the following:

"Slayter [my middle name], good routine, good thoughts, lots of trust! Knock 'em in, Brad Faxon."

This advice has been very helpful to me in tournament play, and I often refer back to it for inspiration. Each of the three keys to his message are encouraging, but the most critical is Brad's advice to have "good thoughts." That in itself is a life lesson—have good thoughts, be positive, and good results will always follow.

Hilary LUNKE

2003 U.S. Women's Open Champion

The best golf advice I've ever received is to "putt like you're blind." It sounds strange, but it really works. If you think about it, blind golfers rely on someone else to line them up, and then they make the same stroke every single time. Whether the putt is dead straight or breaks three feet from left to right, a blind person will make the same stroke. But golfers who can see think some putts are easier than others and put different strokes on different putts. An inconsistent stroke leads to inconsistent results. So when I play, I try to line myself up correctly and then just stroke it down that line every single time, no matter how the putt breaks. Sometimes I'll actually even close my eyes right before I putt to get the sensation. Try that as a drill when you practice—it'll feel really strange at first, but you won't believe how much better you'll start putting.

Angelo R. MOZILO

Vice Chairman and CEO,
Countrywide Financial Corporation

The best putting advice I ever received was the following:

- *Line* up the putt.
- *Lock* in the line.
- *Stroke* the putter and keep your head over the spot of the ball.
- *Listen* for the ball to go into the cup.

Bottom line to remember when putting: line up, lock, stroke, and listen.

Catrin NILSMARK

LPGA Tour Player
2003 and 2005 European Solheim Cup Captain

Aim the putter before you build your stance.

Most golfers miss more putts than they should because they are not disciplined enough in their preparation. The key to holing the ten-footers that the pros make so often is to take a little extra time in carefully aiming the putter face. Most club golfers I know don't even have a routine for aiming the putter. This is crazy when you consider that the hole is just a few inches wide. You can't afford that type of complacency.

I constantly look up and down the line of the putt as I set the putter face behind the ball. I do all of this before I even think about forming my stance for the simple reason that it is much easier to aim the blade accurately before you settle into your address position.

Lana ORTEGA

Director of Instruction, McGetrick Golf Academy
Golf for Women *Magazine Top 50 Teacher*

Putting is the part of golf that presents the greatest opportunity to reduce your scores, yet many golfers waste too many strokes by three-putting. They concentrate too much on the mechanics of their stroke and the line of the putt, and not enough on getting a good feel for distance—especially when you consider that only 48 percent of tour players make putts from six feet, and dramatically fewer as the ball moves farther from the hole.

I was told to use my eyes to gauge the distance of my putts to improve distance control on the putting green. My pre-putt routine incorporates a few realistic practice swings while looking at the hole to let my eyes tell my muscles how much arm swing a particular putt requires. Looking at the hole while making practice swings also helps create a stroke with even rhythm and even length back and through—key factors not only in distance control, but in keeping the putter square throughout the stroke.

Get a feel for the distance

To have good distance control, you must first decide whether you intend to run the ball a foot or two past the hole if it doesn't go in, or just roll the ball over the front edge of the cup. The circumstances of the putt should dictate your approach. For example, it's best to let your eyes focus on the back of the hole on short putts and on uphill putts. On longer "lag" putts, or on fast downhill putts, it's best to bring your attention to a spot short of the hole so that the ball dies over the front edge of the cup. That way you'll leave a tap-in if you don't make your first attempt. Using a quiet mind and letting your eyes tell you how much arm swing is required will help you match your swing with the distance you want to produce.

Jim RITTS

Former Commissioner, LPGA
President and CEO, Primedia Television Group

Many years ago, and long before I became a part of the golf industry as LPGA commissioner, I actually had the opportunity to play quite a bit of golf.

Despite an obvious lack of natural golfing talent, I somehow managed to become a low-single-digit player. Putting, though, was always the weak link of my game. Specifically, I habitually moved my head and eyes just prior to contact during my putting stroke. After years of observing this obvious flaw, a very accomplished amateur player and even better friend, Ed Winter, could no longer stand it. On the practice green one day at Holston Hills Country Club in Knoxville, Tennessee (a wonderful traditionally designed Donald Ross course), Ed walked over to me, dropped a dime on the putting surface, and placed a golf ball on top of the coin. He simply said, "Strike the ball, and at the same time tell me whether the dime reads heads or tails." I did so, as instructed, and made very solid contact. I repeated the drill ten to fifteen times. Miraculously, a lifelong putting problem was cured in less than ten minutes. As I said, I received this advice more than twenty years ago. My single-digit handicap is a distant memory, but thanks to this tip I can still to this day get it up and down from just about anywhere.

Laird SMALL

Director, Pebble Beach Golf Academy
Golf Magazine *Top 100 Teacher*
Golf Digest *Top 50 Teacher*

One of the best pieces of golfing advice I ever heard came from the esteemed golfing professional, Paul Azinger. It came several years ago when I was working with a student just prior to a major tournament. As the tournament's first round was approaching, the student started to miss short putts in the three-to-six-foot range. He was very concerned about the greens on this particular course. They were uneven and full of perceived perils. Azinger, who had only recently completed a successful round of chemotherapy and was all too familiar with challenges both on and off the golf course, stood nearby and took note of the young man's apprehension as he nervously practiced his putting. Paul asked if he could contribute an idea to the lesson that had proved to be very successful to him over the past year and was instrumental to his winning the Hawaiian Open.

> **Swing freely and don't think about the consequences**

Paul told the story of how when you are playing with your friends and you don't make the first putt, the group says, "Pick it up. It's good." The golfer out of habit always goes over and strikes the putt—sometimes backhanded—and it always seems to go in. Paul said that a good part of his success last year was due to saying this to himself before striking his putts: "Pick it up. It's good." It allowed him the freedom to swing the putter freely and not worry about the consequences of missing. He felt this thinking allowed him to make more than his share of putts. He then said that he has taken this same thought back to the fairway and applied it to a five-iron shot to the green. Wow! What a sense of confidence and freedom this can create in a player's mind.

The lesson was immediately clear to my student: This simple thought created extraordinary performance. Those five little words become transformational. They create a metamorphosis of the mind; the attitude changes, allowing the true athlete to come out. These five simple words work on the putting green, they work on the tee, and they work in life: "Pick it up. It's good."

Ken STILL

Former PGA Tour Player

I was on the putting green at the Memphis Open in 1967. Arnold Palmer walked by and asked, "Can I give you a tip?" I replied, "What are you waiting for?" He said, "You're a tap putter, which means your putter stops at the ball with no follow-through." I asked Arnold how to stop this. He said to feel like you're stroking the front of the ball, which makes you follow through. Thirty-eight years later, I still do this when putting. Great tip that I'll never forget.

Chip THOMSON

PGA Tour Instructor
Founder, Blue Chip Promotions

As an instructor for players on the PGA Tour the last several years, I've found that there is no better golf advice than what Harvey Penick told me years ago: "Keep it simple and repeatable." Where most golf instructors will break the swing down in many steps, cluttering the pupil's brain with seemingly complicated swing thoughts, Mr. Penick would say one thing, like "Clip the tee." He could have said, "Grip the club lightly, keep the club in front of you, hold the angle of the wrists as long as you can to create a late hit, stay behind the ball, and hit through the ball with the right arm overtaking the left at impact." Instead of "To hit the ball high, finish high," he could have said, "Pick the club up quickly on the backswing, create a very steep angle of attack to the ball, stay well behind the ball, bring the club up quickly after impact. . . ." He was the master of simplicity and the greatest golf instructor I've ever spoken to or read.

The largest percentage of my teaching is in the short-game area, and the number one fault by amateurs and tour players is alignment. In putting, especially, most players' shoulders and forearms are not aligned, and both are crucial

Proper alignment is key to a good putt

to a repeatable putting stroke. All of our lives, in almost any sport we've played, we face the target. In football, base-ball, bowling—anything target oriented—we face the target. Now, with the most target-intensive thing we've ever done —put a ball in a small hole—we're supposed to stand side-ways and stay there throughout the stroke. It doesn't feel natural, and when the pressure's on, we want to help it by opening up. This forces the right shoulder to come around the left, instead of underneath it, creating an outside-in stroke.

All great putters have had the following fundamentals:

- Shoulders aligned
- Forearms aligned
- Legs fairly straight and bend at the waist so the shoulders rotate "down the line, not across it"
- Hands slightly ahead of the ball throughout the stroke

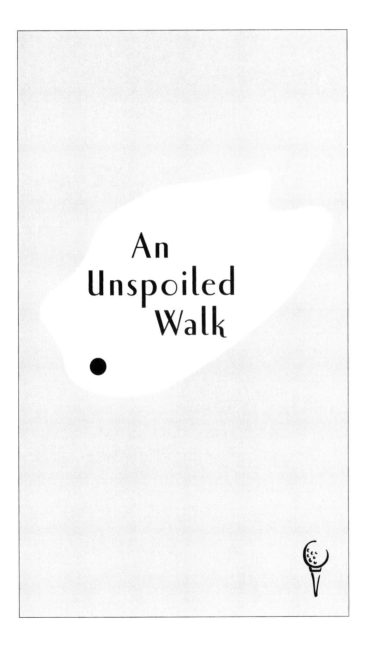

An
Unspoiled
Walk

Amy ALCOTT

1980 U.S. Women's Open Champion
Three-Time Nabisco-Kraft Champion
World Golf Hall of Fame

It's a game—just *play* it.

My best golf has come out of the thought to put more play into everything instead of trying to control or master the game.

Larry BROWN

Head Coach, NBA World Champion Detroit Pistons

The best golf advice I ever received was to enjoy it and not get carried away with trying to be great.

I'm highly competitive. I once threw a golf club when I was an assistant coach at North Carolina. It landed about forty feet away in a pine tree, and I'm shaking the pine tree and all the sap is falling on me while people are walking around. That was the last time I ever threw a club.

Eddie Merrins, who was the golf pro at the Bel-Air Country Club for some thirty-five years, was the golf coach when I was at UCLA. He's really been helpful to me. He tries to keep it simple, and that's what I've tried to do. He's got a theory about swinging the handle. That's one of the big things he always talks to me about. If you swing the handle and concentrate on that, it takes a lot of the other thought processes away. Usually when I concentrate on that, I play a little better. He's a great old man who loves the game, and he's always made it fun for me.

Steve COHEN

Founder and President, Shivas Irons Society
(whose mission is "to explore golf's beauty and mystery,
and to provide opportunities for personal and
social transformation")
Coleader, Golf in the Kingdom Workshops at
Esalen Institute in Big Sur, California

The most useful bit of advice I have been given about golf—the one that I have been most dedicated to following, and the one that I have most often passed on to others—had nothing to do with my performance as a golfer, but rather my performance as the parent of a golfer.

My seven-year-old son Michael had just developed a passionate interest in golf. Anything that involved an orb or a stick or a racket consumed him. Much to my delight, his enthusiasm had turned to the sport that I had only recently rediscovered after many years with my own passion. This was when I turned to Fred Shoemaker for "advice."

Fred is a brilliant golf coach (and a remarkably talented player) whom I had come to know both personally and professionally through our collaboration in leading Golf in the Kingdom workshops at Esalen Institute in Big Sur, California.

I approached Fred for his opinion on Michael's golf education with the hope that he would simply choose to become his mentor. But asking Fred for advice is like it might have been to ask Socrates. The dialogue began something like this:

Don't give advice unless you're asked for it

Steve: Any thoughts about finding a coach for Michael?

Fred: Why do you think he needs a coach?

S: So that he can develop as a player.

F: Has Mike asked for this help?

S: No, he's just interested in playing or hitting balls at the practice tee.

F: How's his game? Has he been improving without a coach?

S: For a seven-year-old, his game is great. And yes, he's been getting better all the time. I want to make sure that this continues.

F: What makes you think it won't?

S: I don't know. I never thought about it in these terms.

F: Does he enjoy himself on the course? Does he get upset when he misses shots?

S: Yes, on both counts. He gets upset, but he

seems to let it go by the time he is ready for the next shot.

F: How do you feel when he gets upset? What do you do?

S: I usually feel empathetic and protective. Sometimes I remind him that he shouldn't expect to be perfect. Everyone misses shots sometimes.

F: Does the reminder help?

S: No, it often makes things worse.

F: What do you imagine would happen if you just left him alone with his "upset"?

And so it went—becoming clearer and clearer to me that I was probably looking more for something to satisfy my own needs than those of my son. After all, his requirements were pretty simple—a place to practice and play and access to some equipment that fit him. Without ever having taken a how-to lesson, Michael had already developed a pretty efficient golf swing, and there was nothing broken that needed fixing. He enjoyed the game and expected to do well whenever he played. His optimism was imperturbable. Especially when I stayed out of his way and didn't lay my expectations on him.

I made an agreement with Michael that I would offer no teaching or coaching unless I was asked. I told him that if he wanted to work with a professional it would be his choice, not mine. Fred, whom he trusted and admired, let him know that he was available.

As for me, I had the pleasure of watching Michael develop into a fine golfer, who, by the time he was a teenager, could easily outdrive and outscore me. By age fifteen, he was close to scratch, and his leadership skills had earned him the captaincy of his high school squad. He participated in a number of junior golf tournaments, had both victories and disappointments, and gave me the proudest moments with the recognition he received as an athlete who was a scholar and a leader.

I will not pretend that we did not have our share of father-son angst during those teenage years, or that there weren't times when I wondered what his game might have been like if he had chosen to take greater advantage of his access to Fred, but in the end I am convinced that taking Fred's "advice" and supporting Michael's independent approach to learning served us both well. For him there is a self-sufficiency that continues to pay dividends in both his personal and professional life, and for me there is a healthy and thriving parental relationship. Michael still loves golf but is not consumed by it. The golf course remains a common ground for us where we can share our love while we appreciate our differences. I approach the game as a laboratory for learning, where my relationship to the score is the most important thing, and he just wants to play golf and shoot the best score he can.

And we both avoid giving advice unless we are asked. Usually.

Cathy Lee CROSBY

Actress and Athlete

It all started in Hawaii when a group of friends invited me to play on a beautiful course there. Having played tennis internationally, achieving a ranking as high as number seven in singles, I figured that even though I'd never even held a club, it would be a snap.

I soon learned that ego and will played no part of this fascinating new game . . . at least in comparison to other more "active" sports I had played. After a rather long period of obvious frustration, a member of our group who had a 2 handicap whispered in my ear, "Relax, let the club do the work, and be at one with the ball." That advice has served me well not only in golf, but in life.

Robert DEDMAN Jr.

CEO, ClubCorp

The best golf advice I ever received was from my father, Robert H. Dedman Sr., who always encouraged me to play G.O.L.F.—Game Of Lifetime Fun. It is a sport that not only builds character but reveals character. He always believed that golf instills meaningful lifetime values like "play it as it lies." Golf has taught me a lot about triumph and disaster and how to treat the twin impostors with equanimity. Another important lesson he taught me was to cherish the relationships you develop on the golf course. Golfers are kindred spirits, and the relationships established through golf will last a lifetime. My father passed away two years ago, but some of my fondest memories are of time we shared together on the eighteenth hole of Pinehurst Number 2 and the Ryder Cup lounge afterwards.

Jim DODSON

Author, Final Rounds, The Dewsweepers,
A Golfer's Life (*with Arnold Palmer*), *and*
Ben Hogan: An American Life
Columnist, Golf Magazine

Even late in life, my dad was urging me to "putt like a kid," meaning to look once and let the putt go with a fairly quick and easy confidence, worrying far less about technique and line than the pleasure of just stepping up and rapping the ball toward the hole—letting it go with minimal fuss. Everyone has had this experience—of just looking, and rapping a ball toward the cup, only to have it dive straight in. Doing this often puts a beautiful roll on the ball because it is naturally relaxed.

"Putt like a kid" leads me to the best philosophical advice about golf I ever received—"play as if it doesn't matter."

Oddly enough, this comes to me via Arnold Palmer and Ben Hogan, having studied their lives and playing styles in great detail. Palmer was routinely criticized for "blowing" several major championships (notably three U.S. Opens and a PGA he all but had his hands around) due to his patented aggressive style of play. But, as he told me while we were working together on his memoirs, that's the best way he knew how to play—a style that had been natural to him since he was a boy, and the key to how he won anything at all.

Play like a kid

"When I'm playing my best," he once told me during a casual round at Latrobe, "it doesn't matter if it's a round with a friend or a golf tournament. I'm playing just the way I feel most comfortable."

He means that he is basically blocking out the world's distractions and not being attached to (or worrying about) the outcome—the plague of all players trying to post a score.

No game is more ruled by emotions than golf and a golf swing is dramatically altered by a mind cluttered by desire and expectation. Ben Hogan had to conquer this very thing in order to finally break through and win. After a decade of near misses, getting close but failing to win, and often choking at the end, his wife, Valerie, gave him a bit of obvious advice that transformed his career. She suggested he find a way to completely block out the world at large and concentrate on hitting shots the way he would when he was practicing (his greatest love)—which eventually permitted him to develop the protective cocoon of silence and almost yogic concentration he was famous for.

That little bit of advice—playing as if it really didn't matter, focusing only on hitting each shot the way that is most natural and pleasurable for you—eliminates dangerous tension and expectations and lets the game flow, and the outcome takes care of itself.

Perry DYE

Founder, Dye Designs (designed more than fifty golf courses in ten states and nine foreign countries, including Cotton Ranch in Colorado; Promontory in Utah; The Wolf at Las Vegas Paiute Resorts)

The advice on golf course design that has stuck in my mind for many years came from Tommy Jacobsen in the mid-1980s when we were building the Farms, an exclusive private club in Rancho Santa Fe, California. I was working on the back tees of a par-4 hole, pushing the tee farther and farther into the cart staging area, when Tommy came up and asked me what I was doing. I told him I was trying to get a little more distance on the hole.

Design for private club members, not professionals

Tommy said, in his very commanding voice, "Perry, private club members don't hit that far. Who are you building the golf course for?"

Even though we now have "supersonic" golf equipment that enables golfers to hit incredibly long shots, I design with the concept that modern golf courses should be built for average golfers.

My passion for working in the golf industry has also endured thanks to advice given me by my father, Pete Dye. He always told me, "If you do what you love, you'll love what you do."

Scott FARMER

CEO, Cintas Corporation

I've received all kinds of advice over the years regarding all aspects of the game. There are countless tips on the grip, club position, posture, and on and on. There has also been a lot of advice on various aspects of the mental side of the game as well. But perhaps the best advice I've ever received about the game of golf came from a very good friend of mine who loves the game.

He said, "We all play the game for any number of reasons, and on the surface everybody's reasons may change from round to round. But at the end of the day, there are only two reasons to play golf. The first is who you play with. This is really what the game of golf is all about. And since it's human nature to be competitive, the second reason is who you play against and what is at stake."

With limited time to play these days, this advice makes the most of each opportunity to play golf.

Angela JERMAN

LPGA Tour Player

I have been very fortunate throughout my life to be surrounded by key individuals who have helped shape my career. They have taught me many incredible life lessons, but two people in particular have affected my golf career more than any others. Their words of encouragement and instruction I carry with me every time I hit the links.

One of my first golf coaches, Bill Godwin, had the motto "Remember to have fun, get a good education, be a good citizen, and hang in there." On the course, there are significant obstacles that I must overcome, but I have found that if I follow his simple advice, everything seems to work out. If I don't have fun on the course, then rounds have a tendency to get away. Earning my education has allowed me to mature as a player and is one of the main reasons I am where I am today. Coach was always tough on me to strive to do my best, but his subtle words are what stick with me day in and day out on the golf course.

You are not defined by your score

The other piece of advice that I carry with me throughout the good, the bad, and the ugly rounds comes from my father. He has always preached to me that "I am not my score." He constantly stresses that my score does not dictate who I am as a person, but rather measures the number of times it took me to get around the golf course. This is a piece of advice that I utilize a lot throughout the year because, regardless of whether I am playing well or playing poorly, I am and always will be just Angela.

Nancy LOPEZ

Forty-eight LPGA Tour Titles
Three-Time Vare Trophy Winner
World Golf Hall of Fame

The best golf advice I ever received was from my wonderful father, Domingo Lopez. It is short and sweet and absolutely true. Since I was eight years old, I've been playing golf, and the one thing my father insisted I do was to play happy. If you're not enjoying yourself out there, you aren't going to get very far. He told me I'd only be great if I loved the game.

Kevin McHALE

Head Coach, Minnesota Timberwolves
Boston Celtics, 1980–1993
Basketball Hall of Fame
Selected as One of the 50 Greatest Players
in NBA History

Work hard at your game, but accept the fact that it's not your primary job and know that you are only going to get so good. Have fun being the best part-time golfer you can be. Remember, 8 or 9 handicaps win most of the money.

Greg MADDUX

Chicago Cubs
Future Hall of Famer

The best advice I ever got was to respect the game and enjoy it. I think once I started doing that I began enjoying the game. I usually play with people better than me, and I usually get a tip a round. That makes it easier to accept their advice.

Jeff MAGGERT

Two PGA Tour Titles

The best advice I ever got was to always have fun. It's a great game, and you don't always have your best day, but you can always enjoy every round. I think every teacher or coach I ever had felt that way.

Phil MICKELSON

2004 Masters Champion
Twenty-five PGA Tour Titles
Four-Time Ryder Cup Team Member
U.S. Amateur Champion—1990
Three-Time NCAA Champion and Player of the Year

My dad gave me the best golf advice I ever received, which was to have fun. That's the reason why, when I practice, I'm always having fun and enjoying it. There have been days when I have driven to the course and turned around and gone home because I didn't feel like playing that particular day. It's why I periodically take two or three weeks off the PGA Tour schedule, to refresh myself and get to where I'm eager to have fun competing again. Every time I'm on the golf course I'm looking forward to being there, I want to be there, and I'm enjoying accomplishing something.

Jim NANTZ

Host, CBS Sports Golf Telecasts

The best golf advice I've received came not in the form of words, but in the actions of my father.

My passion for golf came from my father. Thanks to him, I fell in love with the integrity of the game long before I became enchanted with playing the sport. My father let me tag along with him during his weekend rounds. I watched his every move. I watched with awe his meticulous ways and the manner in which he conducted himself. No one cherished the rules more.

> Golf is a game of honesty and integrity

Etiquette? Forget it. All the great virtues of golf were honored with great relish. I can recall his playing companions always remarking about "Honest Jim."

That was the hook for me. I witnessed the respect people gave my father, and I wanted to be just like him. Of course, with age you learn that golf really is synonymous with doing things the right way. Golf is honesty; honesty is golf.

Dan PASQUARIELLO

Director of Instruction, Pebble Beach Resorts

After teaching golf to more than a hundred thousand students around the world in my thirty-four years in the golf business, I could offer many pearls of wisdom on "how to" swing a golf club. But what I see from students around the globe is their ability, or lack thereof, to have any semblance of consistency. So what I'm about to say is more of a mind-set issue than a swing tip.

> **Learn from the past, don't dwell in it**

Golf is a game of opposites: swing easy to hit it far, swing down to get the ball up, effortless power versus powerless effort. It is a learned, acquired skill versus a natural, instinctive skill. This is the most counterintuitive exercise you will ever attempt. Unlike my wife and automobile, I want my students to have a low-maintenance, high-performance golf swing that will repeat, especially under pressure. Most golfers are too concerned with their *stylish* golf swing and never find their *efficient* golf swing!

We must evaluate why we play golf. Golf is a game. Games are supposed to be fun! Therefore, golf is fun! If you aren't having fun on the golf course, then maybe you should go back to work and make money, or fire someone. In order to enjoy golf, think of the worst thing that could happen if you shot a high score, and the best thing that could happen if you shot a low score. Live in the present, enjoy the moment, and take what the golf gods give you. In other words, the past is history, the future a mystery. Enjoy the moment; it's a gift, that's why they call it the present— the past is to learn from, not to live in!

Roger RULEWICH

*Chief Golf Course Architect, Roger Rulewich Group
(designed and remodeled more than 150 courses in
fourteen countries on five continents)
Former president, American Society of Golf Course
Architects*

Golf course architects survive on their own wits and creativity. Since this type of design isn't taught or learned in any school, the education of an architect is a process of osmosis. This often takes the form of advice from your mentor, from your clients, from builders, and even from other golfers. The trick is to absorb it all and have the good judgment to separate the wheat from the chaff.

Having a famous mentor like Robert Trent Jones for so long, I got advice like "always be ready for any occasion with a coat and tie"; in dealing with important clients, always go to the "horse's head, not the horse's ass"; and it's always better to "ask for forgiveness than to ask for permission." Funny, but I've seen all of it backfire! Every hole a "hard par, easy

A good course is both challenging and accessible

bogey" was a precept repeatedly attributed to Jones. He would admit that variety in a course demanded more than that. But the point he made stuck with me—a course must both challenge the better player and be accessible and fun for the average player.

From a client who advised making "wide fairways" to avoid difficulty, to the one who asked why I was clearing a hole so wide when "the ball is only 1.68 inches in diameter," I've heard it all. The best advice ever from a club member, seeing me begin to compromise on a design issue, was "You might as well fall flat on your face as lean over too far backward."

"Practice makes perfect" doesn't work for sex, child rearing, or even playing golf, but experience for the architect is a great teacher. A well-known golf writer suggested that "every course should give the architect a chance to come back since they can't be expected to get it right the first time." However true, no architect wants to suggest this to those paying the bills. Perhaps the best advice, from another famous architect, that is my constant guide when creating a golf hole is "first make it true to the test of the game and second make it as beautiful as possible."

John SUTTER

PGA Head Professional, Spring Rock Golf Center, New Hyde Park, New York

The best golf advice I ever received was given to me by my father, and I pass it on to you.

In one of his typical wordplays, he talks about golf playing: "Golf is a recreation. So don't wreck the creation."

This phrase has come to me many times on the golf course and practice tee, filling me with a sense of relaxation and confidence. It has allowed me to have more fun, to persevere, and to win. For this, I thank my father.

> **Be your own tough mental coach**

The first part of the statement reminds us that golf is a game—healthy and fun. Sometimes we need to remind ourselves of that. The second part of this saying, "So don't wreck the creation," is funny and profound. It implies that the creation is a force or energy that exists for us. It is our energy and God-given ability that we shouldn't wreck with negative thought or fearful thoughts.

Remembering such a phrase can help us banish negative thoughts and set our minds right to achieve on the golf course, as well as enjoy our time there. My father also used to say, "Play with expectations and enthusiasm on the golf course and demand things of yourself."

Golf is such a personal game that we need this internal dialogue to psych ourselves up to win and not give in to the bogeymen of defeat and lackluster performance. We need to be our own tough coach in golf—summoning courage and demanding things of ourselves in order to win.

So, my advice to play better golf would be three things:

1. Golf is a recreation, so have fun.
2. Play with enthusiasm. Thrive on the energy.
3. Be your own hard-driving coach and demand things of yourself on the golf course.

These are the prescriptions for the golf blues—if you get them.

About the Author

DONALD J. TRUMP is known worldwide for his business acumen, and for his love of golf. His portfolio of golf holdings includes Trump National Golf Club in Westchester, New York, and the Trump International Golf Club in Palm Beach, Florida. Both courses were designed by Jim Fazio and each rated as the number one course in its area. Additionally, the Trump National Golf Club in Bedminster, New Jersey, designed by Tom Fazio, is said to be one of the best courses built in the last twenty-five years. Mr. Trump has also just opened Trump National Golf Club in Palos Verdes, which was designed by Pete Dye and fronts on two miles of the Pacific Ocean. It is, in Mr. Trump's estimation, the best course in the state of California.